AN UNSPEAKABLE CRIME

THE PROSECUTION AND PERSECUTION OF LEO FRANK

ELAINE
MARIE
ALPHIN

CAROLRHODA BOOKS
MINNEAPOLIS / NEW YORK

Carolrhoda Books
A division of Lerner Publishing Group, Inc.
241 First Avenue North
Minneapolis, MN 55401 U.S.A.

Website address: www.lernerbooks.com

Library of Congress Cataloging-in-Publication Data

Alphin, Elaine Marie.
    An unspeakable crime : the prosecution and persecution of
  Leo Frank / by Elaine Marie Alphin.
      p.   cm.
    Incluces bibliographical references and index.
    ISBN: 978-0-8225-8944-0 (lib. bdg. : alk. paper)
    1. Murder—Georgia—Atlanta—Case studies. 2. Trials
  (Murder)—Georgia—Atlanta. 3. Lynching—Georgia—
  Atlanta—Case studies. 4. Phagan, Mary, d. 1913. 5. Frank,
  Leo, 1884–1915. I. Title.
  HV6534.A7A57 2010
  364.152'3092—dc22   2008042300

Manufactured in the United States of America
1 – JR – 12/15/2009

FOR ART,

who cannot witness injustice without speaking up, and who will never endure the companionship of an accusing conscience

CONTENTS

"DIMPLES IN HER CHEEKS"

MARY PHAGAN

Thirteen-year-old Mary Phagan lived in the poor section of Atlanta, Georgia, but she dressed up like a high-society girl on the morning of Saturday, April 26, 1913, Confederate Memorial Day. Even though the War Between the States had been fought thirty-five years before her birth, Mary was excited to celebrate the event. There would be a parade and fireworks, and rumor had it that the widow of the great Confederate general Stonewall Jackson would actually attend!

After doing her morning chores and eating a breakfast of leftover cabbage and bread, Mary put on a pretty store-bought violet dress that accentuated her already well-developed figure. This was a holiday—a day when a little innocent flirting with boys would be fun. She carefully fixed a pair of bows in her thick auburn hair and then topped off the outfit with a blue straw hat that brought out the blue in her bright eyes. Her mother stood on the front porch watching Mary go and noticed her daughter's excitement: "She had dimples in her cheeks."

Clutching her silver mesh purse and a black parasol, Mary hurried through misty rain to catch the streetcar at 11:45. Sixteen-year-old Helen Ferguson remembered waving at Mary as Mary rode toward town. And George Epps, a fifteen-year-old newsboy, said he'd talked to her on the streetcar about watching the parade together.

But Mary had to make one stop before she could celebrate: she had to pick up her pay. Mary worked at the National Pencil Company with more than a hundred other teenage girls. Because of a supply

A photograph of Mary Phagan taken a short time before her death.

A scene from a Confederate Memorial Day parade in Atlanta, Georgia. Mary Phagan had planned to attend the parade on the day of her murder.

shortage of metal used to make pencil caps, she had only worked two shifts during the past week, but Mary wanted the $1.20 she had earned. Around noon that Saturday, she crossed beneath the granite facade of the National Pencil Company building to enter the factory.

Mary Phagan never left the building alive.

And she was not the only person to die.

"THE MURDER OF MARY PHAGAN MUST BE PAID FOR IN BLOOD"

DISCOVERING THE BODY

Seventeen-year-old Grace Hicks worked at the National Pencil Company. She'd enjoyed herself at Saturday's parade and was surprised when her policeman brother-in-law, W. W. "Boots" Rogers, telephoned her early Sunday morning. He told her that the police had found a body in the factory basement, and it was in such terrible condition that no one could identify it. Perhaps Grace might recognize the girl.

Boots Rogers picked up Grace around 4:30 A.M. He drove back to the factory and led Grace through the trapdoor to the basement, where she identified the body as Mary Phagan, who worked with her in the metal department.

Shocked at the sight, Grace later said that Mary "was bruised, in the face somewhere, and one of her teeth was knocked out." Grace thought Mary "looked like she had been hit with something right there," pointing at her own face. "It was bruised, and a hole in her head, here. She had shavings all in her hair." She said Mary's face "was mighty near black" with some sort of dirt or cinders. Grace couldn't bear to look any longer. "It scared me."

The National Pencil Company factory in Atlanta, Georgia. Mary Phagan's body was found in the basement of this building.

The police wanted to notify Mary's family. Grace didn't know how to contact them, but she thought Helen Ferguson, another girl who worked at the factory, might know. When they called Helen from the factory office, she said that Mary's family was too poor to afford a telephone. She volunteered to tell her friend's mother and stepfather in person.

The news would not come as a complete surprise, as Mary's parents had waited up for her all night.

After Mary's father had died in Marietta, where Mary had been born, her mother married John Coleman and they raised Mary in Atlanta. Frannie Coleman had been so worried when Mary hadn't come home Saturday night that she'd sent her husband to town to look for her, thinking that Mary might have gone to the movies. John Coleman searched for nearly three hours. Then he came home and started knocking on neighbors' doors before using a friend's phone to call police after midnight.

Around 5:30 A.M., John and Frannie Coleman learned what had happened to Mary when Helen knocked on their door. Mary's mother collapsed in shock at the description of her daughter's death.

At least she found out before the morning edition of the *Atlanta Constitution* splashed the news of Mary's murder across its front page. Reporter Britt Craig had been in the police station when the telephone rang at 3:30 Sunday morning. "A white woman has been killed up here," said Newt Lee, the National Pencil Company's elderly, African American night watchman.

Britt followed the police to the factory and climbed through the trapdoor into the basement, stumbling through the smoky darkness behind the officers. "Look out, white folks," warned Newt Lee, "you'll step on her."

Neither Britt nor the policemen were surprised to hear Newt Lee call them "white folks." In 1913 Georgia, this form of address would have been considered a mark of respect from a black man who knew his place: below the whites who were in charge. The men stopped and shone their flashlights where Newt pointed. Britt could see a girl lying on the rubbish-strewn earthen floor, partially hidden beside a storage shed.

The officers gently turned the body over and were shocked to see a cord cutting deeply into her throat. Her swollen tongue bulged out from a mouth choked with cinders and sawdust and stained with blood. One shoulder had been bitten. Her dress was pushed up above her knees, and the men saw blood that indicated the girl might have been "criminally assaulted," or "outraged"—1913 euphemisms for rape.

Britt was as angry as the officers that a young girl in a party dress lay dead and violated in the dirt of the factory basement. To these men, Mary Phagan was a child who should have been home with her family instead of having to work in a factory—especially one run by a northern businessman, as the National Pencil Company was. Britt took notes as the officers searched the basement.

The men found a sliding wooden door that led to an alley. The door appeared to have been opened recently and then closed again. They also found one of Mary's shoes and a bloody handkerchief. As they raked through the sawdust and litter around the girl, they found a note, scribbled in pencil on a sheet of white lined paper that matched a company notepad that lay nearby. One officer read it aloud:

he said he wood love me land down play like the night witch did it but that long tall black negro did boy his slef

At that, Newt Lee muttered something. The other men thought he said, "White folks, that's me."

Then the police found a second note beside Mary's head. This one was written on a National Pencil Company order sheet:

mam that negro hire down here did this i went to make water and he push me down that hole a long tall negro black that hoo it wase long sleam tall negro i wright while play with me

These notes appeared to have been written very recently and could have been interpreted in two different ways. They might have been written by Mary just before she died, in a last-minute effort to identify her killer. Or they might have been written by the killer, to throw suspicion away from himself and onto someone else. Police records don't indicate exactly what the officers on the scene thought about the notes, but their immediate reaction was to turn on Newt Lee in fury. "You did this," said the sergeant, "or you know who did it."

The night watchman began to shake. He insisted he hadn't done anything. But he was tall and had very dark skin, so to the officers, he looked like the man described in the notes. They also remembered his reaction to the first note. Newt Lee looked like the obvious suspect, and they immediately took him into custody. In 1913 the Atlanta police force was entirely white and, as reporter Harold Ross would later write, "The murder of Mary Phagan was the most brutal crime in the annals of the South. After the unfolding of the details the police did what they always do in Georgia—arrested a Negro."

After the officers on the scene found the notes, Detectives John Starnes and John Black arrived to continue the investigation. While

The two notes discovered near Mary Phagan's body. The top note reads: *"mam that negro hire down here did this i went to make water and he push me down that hole a long tall negro black that hoo it wase long sleam tall negro i wright while play with me."* The bottom note reads: *"he said he wood love me land down play like the night witch did it but that long tall black negro did boy his slef."* The meaning and authenticity of these notes was important to the case.

Britt Craig wrote his news story for the *Atlanta Constitution* and Helen Ferguson went to break the news to Mary's parents, Detective Starnes searched the crime scene. He found Mary's hat in the basement trash pile. He also studied the sliding wooden door more carefully and saw bloody handprints all over it. A metal pipe leaned against the wall nearby, and Starnes thought it might have been used to force the door open. There was no sign of Mary's purse.

Meanwhile, Detective Black was following a hunch. The detective had already provided evidence that had hung several criminals, and he wanted to be the one to find this girl's murderer. He was not satisfied with the idea of the old black man as the killer. As reporter Ross explained, Black and other members of the police realized something "which determined their whole future course of action: The murder of Mary Phagan must be paid for with blood. And a Negro's blood would not suffice."

But if Newt Lee was not to be charged with the crime, who should be?

Something Lee said had bothered Detective Black. Lee claimed that he'd tried to call the factory superintendent, Leo Frank, after he'd found the body. When he got no answer, he called the police. The night watchman might be lying, of course, but if he was telling the truth, why hadn't Leo Frank answered his phone in the middle of the night?

Even more troubling, the police had tried to call Leo Frank after arresting Newt Lee, and there was still no answer. They'd called and awakened other officials of the National Pencil Company with no trouble. Detective Black suspected that Leo Frank's refusal to answer his phone was important to the case.

"HOARSE AND TREMBLING AND NERVOUS AND EXCITED"

CONFUSION

When the telephone rang at 7:00 Sunday morning, twenty-nine-year-old Leo Frank felt a trace of unease. He had dreamed the telephone had rung in the middle of the night, and now its ringing came far too early for a social call. He lifted the receiver reluctantly.

"Is this Mr. Frank, superintendent of the National Pencil Factory?" It was Detective Starnes.

When Leo Frank answered yes, the detective told him he had to come to the factory immediately. Leo objected, saying he hadn't had his breakfast yet, but Starnes insisted he would send a patrol car.

The car arrived quickly, and Leo's wife, Lucille, invited the policemen to enter the home she and Leo shared with her parents. Leo came downstairs, only partially dressed. He questioned Detective Black and Boots Rogers with nervous distress, asking what had happened at the factory and whether the night watchman had reported anything.

Detective Black interrupted him. "Mr. Frank, you had better get your clothes on and let us go to the factory and see what has happened."

Leo Frank in 1915, two years after the death of Mary Phagan.

To the detective, Leo's behavior seemed suspicious as he struggled with his tie. "His voice was hoarse and trembling and nervous and excited," Black recalled. Boots Rogers also thought Leo looked nervous, and his questions were jumpy. But the police officers weren't particularly reassuring. Leo later remembered, "I asked them what the trouble was and the man who I afterwards found out was Detective Black hung his head and didn't say anything."

A four-person conversation that was part of a police investigation should have been simple to document. But the confusion that would mar every step of the attempts to find out what had happened to Mary Phagan began that morning with this initial conversation between the police officers and the Franks. Leo, Lucille, and Boots Rogers recalled that Leo's wife offered everyone coffee, perhaps hoping that southern hospitality would calm the tension. But Detective Black remembered that Leo suggested the coffee. To the detective, it sounded as if the superintendent wanted to delay going to the factory.

Leo recalled that the police asked him, in front of his wife, if he knew Mary Phagan. He told them he didn't. Then they asked, "Didn't a little girl with long hair hanging down her back come up to your office yesterday sometime for her money?" Leo agreed that a girl had indeed come to his office for her pay but said he didn't know her name was Mary Phagan. He had issued the $1.20 she had earned based on her employee number, not her name.

Leo finished dressing and left with the officers, without any breakfast or coffee. All three men agreed that they drove to the mortuary to view the body. Leo recalled looking closely at the girl and identifying her, but both Black and Rogers remembered the superintendent hanging back, then turning away nervously before they left to go to the factory.

Detective Black observed everything Leo did with a suspicious eye. Trying to answer police questions, the superintendent fumbled through pay records to confirm that Mary Phagan was the girl he had paid on Saturday. When asked to take the group down to the basement, Leo asked again for coffee before struggling with the power switch and the cables of the manual elevator. In the end, an

The police station in Atlanta, Georgia, as it was in 1913 at the time of the murder of Mary Phagan. Leo Frank was first questioned at this station.

employee had to work the elevator. Black saw the superintendent's nervousness and his requests for coffee as attempts to delay the moment when he would have to look at the scene of the crime. Once they reached the basement, Black thought it was significant that Leo paid little attention to the sawdust and cinders where police told him the body had lain but was distressed by the forced door with the bloody handprints.

Then they all drove to the police station house, where officers wanted Leo to examine the two notes found beside Mary's body. Despite the mild weather, Leo shivered uncontrollably as he sat in the front seat of the police car, adding to Detective Black's suspicion.

Leo felt he was only reacting naturally to police suspicion and a horrifying murder. Later, he would say,

> *Imagine, awakened out of my sound sleep, and a run down in the cool of the morning in an automobile driven at top speed, without any food or breakfast, rushing into a dark passageway, coming into a darkened room, and then suddenly an electric light flashed on, and to see the sight that was presented by that poor little child; why, it was a sight that was enough to drive a man to distraction. Of course I was nervous; any man would be nervous if he was a man.*

Detective Black felt no sympathy for Leo Frank's nervousness. He knew they needed to arrest a better suspect than Newt Lee quickly, before people criticized a police force that couldn't even find the villain who had attacked and murdered an innocent girl.

As Atlanta's population had gone up, crime had increased. Unable to keep pace, the police force had gotten a reputation for failing to solve crimes. At times they tried to improve their success rate by resorting to brutality to get confessions when solid investigation didn't bring results.

Unfortunately, the police got off to a poor start on this murder case by breaking the chain of evidence from the factory. When Leo arrived at the police station with the officers, there was no sign of the two notes they wanted him to see. The police would later discover that reporter Harold Ross of the *Atlanta Journal* had removed them to use in his paper, trying to make up for missing Britt Craig's scoop in the *Atlanta Constitution*. But in front of Leo, the police acted untroubled by this disappearance, even though the notes had not yet been examined by any expert or even dusted for fingerprints. Chief of Detectives Newport Lanford spoke with Leo briefly and then let him go and turned back to other leads.

While officers interrogated Newt Lee, taking him back and forth between the station house and the factory basement, other detectives followed up a report from Edgar Sentell, a twenty-one-year-old grocery clerk who knew Mary Phagan. Sentell had read Britt Craig's story in the *Constitution*, and told police that he'd seen Mary around 12:30 Saturday night with twenty-four-year-old Arthur Mullinax, a streetcar conductor. That led some officers to a new theory. Perhaps the African American watchman had committed the murder, but not alone. Perhaps he had been paid to do it by a white man.

When police questioned Mullinax, he confessed that he knew Mary and greatly admired her. They had both been in a church play the previous Christmas. Mary had been the star, and Mullinax admitted, "I couldn't keep my eyes off her." With no more substantial evidence than that, police arrested Arthur Mullinax on suspicion of murder. Another questionable lead would prompt them to also arrest James Gantt, a disgruntled former employee of the factory who had come by that Saturday claiming to want some shoes he'd left behind.

But Detective Black wasn't convinced that these new leads were important. That morning he'd observed a nervous, excited man who seemed reluctant to see either the basement site where Mary had been found or the dead girl's body itself. Detective Black needed to know more about the factory superintendent. Who was this Leo Frank?

"THE SOUL OF HONOR"

A YANKEE IN ATLANTA

Leo Frank had lived in Atlanta for nearly five years, but he still felt very much an outsider in the South. Although he was technically a southerner, having been born in Texas, Leo's parents had moved to Brooklyn, New York, in the summer of 1884 when he was only three months old. Rudolph and Rachel Frank had raised Leo as most New York Jewish parents raised their children at the time. He played with friends in the Brooklyn streets, went to the seaside in summer with his family, attended public schools, and played basketball on his high school team (which was undefeated his senior year, even in a game against the Yale University varsity team). He also read voraciously, and his imagination was so fired by the books he read that he named his small fleet of toy sailboats after the characters in James Fenimore Cooper's Leatherstocking Tales series of novels.

After graduating from the Pratt Institute, Leo studied mechanical engineering at Cornell University, where he was active on the debate team and made close friends who called him Max. He had also discovered a fascination with photography and enjoyed taking landscape photos. Morris Clurman wrote that Leo was well thought of "by his fellow students who loved him for his manly qualities, his warm-heartedness and his readiness at all times to help a friend. He was the soul of honor." William Lynn Ransom recalled, "He always impressed me as a quiet, sincere, dependable, substantial and rather matter of fact sort of a fellow with rather emphatic convictions and an absolute loyalty to them and to sound standards of life."

Leo Frank, age 9.

Leo worked as an engineer for B. F. Sturtevant Company in Hyde Park, Massachusetts, after he graduated from Cornell. He missed New York, however, and returned there to work for the National Meter Company. By this time, Rudolph Frank had been forced to retire after a railway accident, and Leo's parents and sister, Marian, were living on the interest from the injury settlement. In 1907 Moses Frank (Leo's uncle and a southerner who had fought for the Confederacy in the Civil War) suggested a way Leo could help the family. Uncle Moses had invested in the National Pencil Company in Atlanta. His engineer nephew, who had a keen understanding of production machinery, looked like just the person to help improve the company.

In preparation for his new job, Leo went to Germany to study pencil manufacturing at Eberhard Faber. Then he moved to Atlanta in 1908 to apply the scientific production methods he had observed abroad. But his new home city was very different from the society he had experienced in New York, Massachusetts, or even Germany. Many southerners lived as much in the past as the present. Although the Civil War had been over for almost fifty years, people kept its memory alive, calling it the War Between the States (stressing their belief in the right of individual states to secede), the War of Northern Aggression or, simply, the Recent Unpleasantness. People who had lived through the war and their descendants honored the soldiers who had fought in it. Celebrations like Confederate Memorial Day mattered equally to older people who had grown up before the war and to young people who had never known the Old South, like Mary Phagan and the other teenagers who worked in the National Pencil Company.

One reason the "unpleasantness" seemed so recent was because the U.S. government's process of bringing the Confederate states back into the Union during Reconstruction felt like an extension of the war to most southerners. During the war, Union soldiers from the North commanded by General William T. Sherman had swept across Georgia to the sea, burning over 80 percent of Atlanta to the ground in their wake. After the peace, northern officials had swept into southern states, determined to suppress not only slavery, but any signs of rebellious thinking. These Yankees levied heavy taxes upon owners of small farms and large plantations alike. Southerners had no way to vote against these taxes, because only politicians approved by the northerners could run for office.

In these circumstances, any northern businessman would be viewed as an outsider and an enemy. Leo, standing only five feet six inches tall and weighing only 120 pounds, could never pass for a typical well-fed, physically fit southern gentleman. With his delicate, fine-boned face; a full, fleshy mouth; and nearsighted eyes that appeared to bulge behind his thick glasses, Leo looked to the people of Atlanta exactly the image of a calculating Yankee.

Nevertheless, Leo was so successful that he was promoted to a directorship, a vice presidency, and the position of factory superintendent. But his professional success did little to help him feel at ease in southern society. People were more formal in their manners than what he had seen in New York. Worried that he might somehow offend someone in this strange new world, Leo carefully considered his every action and word before doing or saying anything, to the point that he appeared stilted and distant.

But Leo worked to make himself at home in Atlanta's Jewish society, and there he was welcomed. Within a week of arriving, Leo was introduced to twenty-year-old Lucille Selig and began courting her. The Seligs were a high-society family in Atlanta's Jewish community, but Leo's letters to Lucille show that he was more in love with the girl than her social status. Generously plump, pretty, dark-haired, and quick-witted, Lucille seemed a good match for Leo, teasing him out of his serious nature and making her affection for him clear. When Valentine's Day came, she showed him how he had captured her heart by giving him a handmade red construction-paper heart displaying his name. On June 14, 1909, just five days after he proposed to her and she accepted his hand in marriage, Leo wrote:

> *Your kindly words for me are much appreciated and are treasured up on the scrolls of memory.*
> *I am not much on the sentimental letter writing. Read between the lines and see if you can feel the warmth of the writer's feelings for you!*

Leo Frank and Lucille Selig in Atlanta, Georgia. Leo was introduced to Lucy shortly after arriving in Atlanta in 1908. They were married in 1910.

*. . . Continue to enjoy yourself, sweet one, and be
assured of a joyous welcome home at the hands of*
Yours for eternal happiness
Leo

Lucille and Leo were married on November 30, 1910, and Lucille admitted that she might be "foolishly fond of him. But he is my husband, and I have the right to love him very much indeed, and I do. If I make too much of him, perhaps it is because he has made too much of me." In the spring of 1913, their married life became even happier when Lucille proudly announced that she was pregnant.

Happy in his marriage and in his work, Leo quickly rose to prominence in Atlanta's Jewish community. He worked with a number of charitable organizations and was elected president of the local B'nai B'rith chapter, a Jewish community service organization. Despite his success with the National Pencil Company and Jewish society, however, Leo was not popular among typical Atlanta citizens.

Many Atlanta citizens had their reasons to dislike everything Leo Frank represented. First of all, he was Jewish. The Old South had not been particularly anti-Semitic, or prejudiced against Jews. In fact, Judah P. Benjamin had risen to the position of attorney general of the Confederacy and then secretary of war. Still, while Atlanta's sizable Jewish population was respected, they were still in the minority, and they were considered "different."

Leo was even more different from other Atlanta Jews because he was both a Yankee and an industrialist. This combination made him an unappealing addition to any southern community. Reconstruction had hit southern farmers and rural workers hard. Many were forced to give up their farms and move to cities where they could find industrial work. Between 1900 and 1913, Atlanta had doubled in population. Newcomers desperately hunted for jobs in the mills and factories. Wages were so low (ten to fifteen cents an hour—only two-thirds of what workers in the North earned) that families had as many members working as possible.

Nearly all the production-line employees at the National Pencil Company were teenagers. Although child labor laws had technically been in existence in some states since 1836, the first federal child labor law would not be written until 1916. That was too late to help Mary Phagan, who had started working in a textile mill when she was only ten years old.

Newspapers fed the resentment that Atlanta readers already felt toward northern-owned factories. The *Atlanta Georgian*, owned by sensationalist publisher William Randolph Hearst, was willing to exploit any issue that would sell papers and, with more passion than accuracy, regularly attacked factory owners. The front page of the Monday morning *Georgian* showed a horrifying photograph of Mary's body on the slab at the undertakers. Five pages of articles were full of

In the weeks after the murder, newspapers published photographs of Mary Phagan's clothes and other evidence found around her body. This photo of the clothes Mary was wearing and of the cord found around her neck was published in the April 30 issue of the *Georgian*.

details about the murder and the family's grief—many of which had been exaggerated (and occasionally invented).

There was no twenty-four-hour cable news coverage in 1913, no Internet blogs or YouTube videos or Twitter updates, but people then had the same fascination with the news as they do today. They learned about the twists and turns in any newsworthy event by buying new editions of the papers. Each newspaper published several editions every day and would strive to sell the most papers by coming up with breaking news and dramatic headlines to capture the reader's attention.

By that afternoon, both the *Atlanta Journal* and the *Atlanta Constitution* were featuring photos of Mary Phagan and presenting the girl as southern womanhood defiled, enslaved by northern industrialization. The *Constitution* offered a reward of one thousand dollars to anyone who'd seen Mary after noon on Saturday.

By the time those afternoon editions hit the streets, a young machinist had made news by shifting the scene of the crime from the basement to the upper floors—near Leo's office.

"I COULD TELL IT WAS BLOOD BY LOOKING AT IT"

INVESTIGATION

When eighteen-year-old Robert Barrett got to work a little after 6:30 Monday morning, he saw a red spot on the floor of the factory's second-story metal department, where Mary Phagan had worked. Robert admitted, "I never searched for any blood spots before, until Miss Jefferson came in and said she understood Mary had been murdered in the metal department, then I started to search right away; that was the only spot I could find; I could tell it was blood by looking at it. I can tell the difference between blood and other substances. I found the hair some few minutes afterward—about 6 or 8 strands of hair and pretty long." He reported his finds to his foreman, Lemmie Quinn, who called the police.

Detective Starnes arrived, surrounded by reporters, to find a group of factory workers crowding around the machine where Barrett worked. Fourteen-year-old Magnolia Kennedy, a metal department worker like Mary, stared at the strands of hair Robert had found twisted around his lathe and announced, "It's Mary's hair. I know it."

Detective Starnes hadn't come alone this time. Police Chief James Litchfield Beavers had realized this case was going to be important to all of Atlanta, so he decided to make sure that the investigation was proceeding correctly. Beavers examined the hairs and had an officer chip out a few pieces of the red-splashed wooden floor so he could test it himself, using a bottle of alcohol. When the color didn't dissolve in the alcohol (not a very scientific test, even in 1913), Chief Beavers announced to the reporters that the substance was blood. This created the suspicion that Mary had been killed near Leo Frank's office and then dragged to the elevator and taken downstairs to the basement.

Reporters, searching for new scoops to fill the pages of those extra editions, eagerly questioned the workers about Mary and about what went on inside the factory. The teenage employees were flattered by the attention, and many of them agreed to be interviewed. Police investigators were equally willing to talk to the press, presenting developing theories as solid information. Newspapers printed more and more editions in the first days after Mary's body was found, whipping their readers into a frenzy with their constantly breaking news.

Detective Black didn't go to the factory with the other policemen. He and another officer went to Leo Frank's house to escort the superintendent back to the police station. As they walked downtown, Leo repeatedly asked why they wanted him. When Black wouldn't answer, the other officer said, "Well, Newt Lee has been saying something."

Finally, they reached the station house. Once again, Leo passed through the marble archway and under the scowling gargoyles that watched over the towering Gothic building. Leo was still waiting to speak with Detective Chief Lanford when Herbert Haas, the National Pencil Company's attorney, arrived.

A few minutes later, Luther Rosser joined Haas. Rosser would act as co-counsel in the case. Rosser handled high-profile corporate cases in Atlanta and was the law partner of Governor-elect John Slaton. Rosser liked to present himself as a robust country boy who rarely wore a tie—something of a diamond in the rough. But he had a reputation as a powerful trial attorney who was a master at cross-examination, a talent that no one expected would be needed at this point.

Busy talking to each other, Rosser and Haas missed Detective Chief Lanford's return and his beckoning of Leo into his office. When they realized Leo was gone, the lawyers became outraged that he was talking to the police without counsel, and Rosser demanded to be allowed to accompany his client.

Chief Lanford was surprised by the lawyer's vehemence. He had simply wanted to ask Leo a few questions about Newt Lee's time slip for his Saturday night rounds. Rosser's outburst seemed overly dramatic since Leo Frank hadn't been charged with anything. Chief Lanford began to wonder why the lawyer was so determined to protect his client.

When Chief Lanford showed the time slip to Leo, Leo noticed that there were problems with it. The watchman should have been punching in regularly as he made his rounds, but he had missed several punches. While this made Newt Lee look more guilty, Chief Lanford now viewed Leo himself with increasing suspicion. He asked Leo repeatedly to clarify his answers about the watchman's job and his own motivations in setting up Newt Lee's schedule on Confederate Memorial Day.

Outraged that police could even consider Leo Frank as a possible suspect, Rosser blustered, "Why, it's preposterous. A man who would have done such a deed must be full of scratches and marks and his clothing must be bloody."

Eager to discourage police suspicion, Leo voluntarily stripped, displaying his unscratched chest and arms. Haas suggested that police should be allowed to inspect the dirty laundry at the Franks' home, and Leo agreed. Detective Black and another officer sorted through all Leo's laundry without finding any blood.

After they left, Leo felt confident that he had allayed suspicions about himself. Now he concentrated on how he could get the case solved quickly so that factory production could return to its normal schedule. He phoned his assistant, Herbert Schiff, and asked him to find outside investigators, preferably Pinkerton detectives. The Pinkertons had a reputation for working for large companies whose owners paid them to do what was best for the company, whether by investigating crimes or breaking strikes.

By Monday afternoon, Leo felt he had protected his company. He sent a telegram to his uncle, assuring him that he had the situation well under control.

But according to the Monday evening and Tuesday morning editions of the newspapers, nothing was under control. Both the *Georgian* and the *Constitution* warned their readers that police claimed they were working around the clock to discover the identity of Mary Phagan's killer but without success. The papers offered new rewards for any additional information.

As Mary Phagan's family buried their daughter on Tuesday morning in her hometown of Marietta, they certainly hoped the

police would soon identify the murderer. The Reverend T. T. G. Linkous prayed over Mary's grave with steadily increasing fervor:

We pray for the police and the detectives of the city of Atlanta. We pray that they may perform their duty and bring the wretch that committed this act to justice. We pray that the authorities apprehend the guilty party or parties and punish them to the full extent of the law. Even that is too good for the imp of Satan that did this. Oh, God, I cannot see how even the devil himself could do such a thing.

"A VICTIM WORTHY TO PAY FOR THE CRIME"

ARREST

Fourteen-year-old Alonzo Mann worked as an office boy at the National Pencil Company. One of his jobs was to bring his boss the morning newspaper. Britt Craig's article on the front page of the Tuesday *Constitution* predicted that Leo Frank would be arrested before the day was over. Alonzo recalled, "I cried when I read the paper before I gave it to Frank. Frank talked to me, telling me always [to] be good as he was in life and that way it would always work out right. Frank could tell I cried."

Not all the newspaper morning editions agreed with Britt Craig. The *Journal* headlines screamed "THREE HANDWRITING EXPERTS SAY NEGRO WROTE THE TWO NOTES FOUND BY BODY OF GIRL" and claimed that Newt Lee's guilt was proven. But Detective Black did not believe that the night watchman could have acted alone to commit this murder. He thought the real culprit was someone who had paid him to write the notes to confuse the police. And he was certain that someone was Leo Frank.

Late Tuesday morning, Black investigated Lee's apartment and found a bloody linen shirt. He thought the shirt looked freshly pressed, suggesting that it hadn't been worn. The blood looked as if it had been rubbed into the fabric, not spattered onto it while someone was wearing it. Black suspected that Leo had offered his own laundry to be searched (even though Haas, not Leo, had made the suggestion) specifically so the police would also search Newt Lee's laundry—and

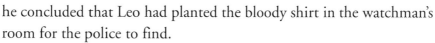

THE ATLANTA GEORGIAN

Read For Profit—GEORGIAN WANT ADS—Use For Results

EXTRA No.6

VOL. XI. NO. 229.   WEATHER: FAIR   ATLANTA, GA., TUESDAY, APRIL 29, 1913   PRICE TWO CENTS

POLICE HAVE THE STRANGLER

USTRIA WILL MOVE ALONE ON MONTENEGRO

DETAILS OF BIG PONY CONTEST ANNOUNCED

VOLS SCORE IN FIRST; BRADY OPPOSES BECK

Late this afternoon, Chief of Detectives Lanford made this important statement to a Georgian reporter: "We have the strangler. In my opinion the crime lies between two men, the negro watchman, Newt Lee and Frank. We have eliminated John Gantt and Arthur Mullinax."

FRANK AND NEGRO ARE GIVEN "THIRD DEGREE"

> **Competing newspapers in Atlanta devoted huge headlines and extra editions to covering Mary Phagan's death and the search for her murderer.**

he concluded that Leo had planted the bloody shirt in the watchman's room for the police to find.

Flushed with certainty that his hunch about Leo Frank was proving correct, Black hurried from Lee's apartment to the station house to place the bloody shirt into evidence. Then he informed reporters that he had a big break in the case at last. He rushed to the factory where the superintendent was trying to get production back to normal, burst into the superintendent's office and proved the *Constitution* right by arresting Leo Frank for the murder of Mary Phagan.

Leo could not believe it. Looking around his office for something normal he could take with him, he saw a box of cigars. A heavy smoker, Leo grabbed a handful of them and stuffed them in his pocket. Perhaps he needed something to remind him that he was an ordinary, innocent citizen as Black triumphantly led him to the police station and confronted him with a piece of the bloody shirt.

Confused, Leo thought they were asking him if the material came from a shirt of his. He said he'd never owned a shirt like that. While police questioned Leo, his lawyer Luther Rosser sped to the station, only to be turned away. People had gathered outside, and an officer stood on the stairs, under orders not to let the crowd interrupt the interrogation. Furious, Rosser had to telephone the chief, demanding to be admitted. As soon as he got upstairs, he upbraided Chief Beavers for trying to keep a lawyer away from his client and then stormed into the interrogation room.

Leo was being questioned by Detective Black—in the presence of Pinkerton detective Harry Scott, who had been put in charge of the National Pencil Company's case. In fact, when Rosser appeared, Black let the Pinkerton detective take over the interrogation.

Leo had hired Pinkertons to protect the reputation of his company. Now one of them was helping the police build a case against him! Leo was unaware that Pinkerton detectives often worked closely with the police on their cases. And he certainly hadn't known that Detective Scott had previously worked closely with Detective Black.

Angry, Leo pointed out, "You were hired by me, if you remember!"

To Leo's surprise, Scott replied, "I was put on the case by my superiors. They were employed to catch the murderer. . . . If you are the murderer, then it's my duty to convict you."

While Leo was being interrogated, his wife hurried to the police station with her father and her brother-in-law. The same police officer who tried to keep Luther Rosser out of the station successfully kept Lucille away from her husband. In the lobby office, crowded by aggressive reporters, Lucille insisted that Leo was innocent and then broke down sobbing.

When Leo heard that his wife was downstairs, in tears, he sent a message telling her to go home, assuring her that he would soon be freed. Lucille left, admitting that she "was humiliated and distressed by numerous people, maybe newspaper reporters, maybe somebody else, snapshotting me with hand cameras."

Soon Atlanta erupted with rumors that Lucille had never come to visit Leo because she knew he was guilty, that she had been in the process of divorcing him at the time of Mary's murder, and that only large sums of money had persuaded her to stay by his side. Later, Lucille would write to the editor of the *Augusta Chronicle*, desperate to expose "that falsehood about my conduct toward the one whom I loved more dearly than my own life, whom I yet love, thank God."

She explained:

> I went to the police station and begged to see him. Think
> of the tender solicitude for me in begging me not to come
> to his cell. He knew he was innocent; I knew he was
> innocent; he expected to be out without delay; he didn't
> want me to see him behind bars. Because he considered
> me, even above himself, he had to bear the burden of
> lies, and I had to bear them. Not a day passed after he
> was taken from home that we did not talk to each other.
> His concern was always for me. "Don't come down here,
> dear" he would say, "I don't want you to remember
> having seen me in this place."

After sending his wife home, Leo's ordeal was far from over. Police had been interrogating Newt Lee, and they decided to put the two men together. Just as Leo was about to lie down on the cot in his cell that night, Black and Scott asked him to talk to Newt Lee. They claimed they wanted him to get the watchman to admit his guilt, and Leo agreed. He remembered Black telling him to tell Lee "that you are here and that he is here and that he better open up and tell all he knows about the happenings at the pencil factory that Saturday night, or you will both go to hell."

Leo entered the interrogation room and did as requested, but Lee insisted he knew nothing to "open up" about. Both Detective Black and Pinkerton detective Scott listened outside the door as the two men talked. Leo used Black's words—but later Black insisted he never told Leo what to say. Scott noticed that Leo was clearly nervous and uncomfortable talking to the watchman. "He was very squirmy in his chair," the Pinkerton detective recalled, "crossing one leg after the other and didn't know where to put his hands; he was moving them up and down his face, and he hung his head a great deal of the time the negro was talking."

Leo had reason to become a good deal more "squirmy" soon. As he was led out of the interrogation room, Leo recalled, Scott and Black went in, "and then began questioning Newt Lee, and then it was that I had my first initiation into the third degree of the Atlanta police department. The way that fellow Black cursed at that poor old Negro, Newt Lee, was something awful. He shrieked at him, he hollered at him, he cursed him, and did everything but beat him." Before this, Leo had believed that cooperating with the police would help them find the real killer and free him. Now he feared it might not work that way.

Newt Lee's continued protestations of innocence under their aggressive questioning convinced both detectives that the night watchman was not guilty of the murder of Mary Phagan. They were equally certain that Leo Frank was the killer. And they could sense that the citizens of Atlanta shared this opinion. Later, the pastor of Mary's Baptist church wrote to a friend, "My feelings, upon the arrest of the old negro watchman, were to the effect that this one old negro would be poor atonement for the life of this innocent girl. But, when on the next day, the police arrested a Jew, and a Yankee Jew at that, all of the inborn prejudice against Jews rose up in a feeling of satisfaction, that here would be a victim worthy to pay for the crime."

First, however, the legal process had to be observed. A coroner's inquest had to officially determine the cause of Mary Phagan's death before the case could be turned over to Solicitor General Hugh Dorsey to prosecute the villain. But for that prosecution to be successful, the police and Dorsey still needed one thing: a motive for the killing.

"MISCONDUCT AT THE FACTORY"

SURPRISES AT THE INQUEST

Fifteen-year-old George Epps waited impatiently through the first part of the coroner's inquest on Wednesday, April 30. The newsboy was eager to testify about seeing Mary on the streetcar the day she was killed. What he had to tell the coroner about a possible motive in Mary's death would shock Atlanta.

A coroner's inquest is a court proceeding to determine the cause of death. Before anyone can be charged with murder, an officer of the court called a coroner must determine whether the victim died of natural causes, accidental causes, or foul play. Coroner Paul Donehoo had six jurors to help him weigh the evidence and settle on a verdict.

The inquest opened with statements from the police officers who had first seen Mary's body in the factory basement. Then Newt Lee testified about finding the body and calling the police, followed by several factory employees. So far the inquest was going as expected. Donehoo was a highly respected officer of the court, one who the people of Atlanta believed brought unusual meaning to the claim

Fifteen-year-old George Epps provided crucial testimony at the coroner's inquest.

"Justice is blind." Paul Donehoo was, indeed, blind. Many people thought his inability to see witnesses helped him do his job, because he listened more carefully.

Donehoo certainly listened carefully to George Epps when the teenager took the stand. George stated that he had ridden on the streetcar with Mary the morning of her death and made a date to watch the parade with her and then go to a movie—after she picked up her pay. Then George announced that the idea of going into the factory to get her pay had frightened Mary, because Leo Frank would be there.

"When she would leave the factory on some afternoons, she said, Frank would rush out in front of her and try to flirt with her as she passed. She told me that he had often winked at her and tried to pay her attention. He would look hard and straight at her, she said, and then would smile. It happened often, she said." George added, "She told me she wanted me to come down to the factory when she got off as often as I could to escort her home and kinder protect her."

This testimony supported the deep-seated resentment so many members of Atlanta's working class felt against northern industrialists. These Yankees had dragged families away from their farms where their daughters were safe and plunged them into city life where young girls had to go to work and risk unwanted sexual advances from bosses or coworkers. When people read the newspaper headlines accusing Leo Frank of flirting with Mary, they were both outraged and titillated. They wanted to hear more about what went on inside this factory.

At first, so did the coroner. The solicitor general, making the case against Leo for the State of Georgia, had subpoenaed many of Mary's fellow employees to testify. But the more Donehoo considered George's testimony and what the other employees might say, the more he feared the inquest was moving too fast. After meeting with chiefs Lanford and Beavers, he adjourned the inquest for a few days. That would allow public outrage to settle down and let the police investigation proceed.

While the police continued their investigation, so did the Pinkerton detectives under Harry Scott. In fact, Scott and Black concentrated their efforts by investigating together. The Pinkertons might have originally been hired by Leo, but they were no longer investigating the case without bias. They were now working with the police specifically to find evidence that would keep their employer behind bars. In fact, Detective Scott told his fellow Pinkertons, "Unless the Jew is convicted, the Pinkerton Detective Agency [will] have to get out of Atlanta."

When the inquest resumed on Monday, May 5, Leo took the stand. Donehoo wanted to get a sense of the superintendent's character. Unlike the shivering, nervous man who had made police so suspicious, the witness who answered the coroner's questions was well dressed and presented a calm, articulate face to jurors and even to reporters. Leo repeated his account of an ordinary work Saturday: he had gotten to his office early; met with his department heads; put the office boy, Alonzo Mann, to work; collected the mail; dictated some letters to his stenographer; spoke to several employees who had come in; seen the office boy and stenographer leave; and given a girl her pay envelope shortly after noon.

Then he had done some paperwork; locked up for lunch while several men continued to work in the factory; eaten lunch with his father-in-law; and walked through town, greeting several employees who were in the crowd watching the parade. He returned to work after deciding not to attend the afternoon baseball game because of rainy weather and then went home to a quiet evening with his family. From the house, he had telephoned night watchman Newt Lee, since the man had only started working for the company two weeks earlier. It was all routine activity, but it left almost an hour unaccounted for between when he paid Mary and when he left for lunch, with no witnesses to confirm that he was working in his office. The police were convinced that Mary Phagan had been murdered during that hour.

After nearly four hours of testimony, Donehoo asked if Leo would like to add anything else about the day. Unexpectedly, Leo said that one of the plant foremen, Lemmie Quinn, had visited him a few minutes after he had paid the girl. Leo had not mentioned this previously, but it gave him an alibi for what had looked like unaccounted-for time.

The coroner was astounded that he could have forgotten something so important, but Leo simply said that speaking with Quinn had slipped his mind until Quinn had mentioned it on Monday, a week ago. Leo chose not to reveal that his lawyers had advised him to save the information for the inquest and say nothing to the police about it, advice he agreed with after seeing the police in action with Newt Lee. To reporters, Quinn confirmed that he had spoken with Leo in his office. Newspapers printed new editions proclaiming "Leo Frank Innocent."

Despite the favorable impact of Leo's testimony, considerable evidence had materialized that made Leo look like a sexual predator who lusted after the young girls he employed. A streetcar conductor found a suspicious note tucked under one of the seats in the same car that Mary had ridden on Saturday. The note claimed that Leo Frank had made numerous sexual advances to Mary. Police asked Helen Ferguson, Mary's friend, to look at the note, which claimed that Mary had told the writer that Leo Frank had put his arm around her and asked if she "wanted to take a joy ride to Heaven." The note claimed that Mary had asked how, and Frank had promised to show her someday. It was signed "A 13-year-old chum of Mary." When Helen read the note, she immediately recognized the handwriting and told police that the letter had actually been written by Grace Hicks, the seventeen-year-old girl who had identified the body.

The idea that something was going on with the factory girls may have had its basis in fact. Helen told Pinkerton agent L. P. Whitfield, "I have not seen any misconduct at the factory lately, but there used to be misconduct during the dinner hour among some of the girl and boy employees. I have never seen anything myself in this connection but have heard of same. Mr. Frank heard of the improper conduct and he endeavored to stop the boys and girls from being together during the dinner hour."

Some of the girls who were interviewed wanted people to think they knew more than they did. Helen also reported, "Grace Hicks was at my house on April 27th, 1913 and she stated that she would tell all she knew about the murder of Mary Phagan, but that she was afraid that the negro Newt Lee, would get out of jail and kill her."

The factory workers who did testify at the inquest were even more outspoken. Fourteen-year-old Nellie Pettis's sister-in-law used to work at the factory, and Nellie had seen Leo a few times. She testified, "I went into the office of Mr. Frank, I asked him for her. He told me I couldn't see her unless I 'saw' him first. I told him I didn't want to 'see him.' He pulled a box from his desk. It had a lot of money in it. He looked at it significantly and then looked at me. When he looked at me, he winked. And as he winked he said: 'How about it?' I instantly told him I was a nice girl."

Another Nellie, sixteen-year-old Nellie Wood, had worked at the factory herself and testified that Leo "asked me one day to come into his office saying that he wanted to talk to me. He tried to close the door, but I wouldn't let him. He got too familiar by getting so close to me. He also put his hands on me."

When the coroner asked where Leo had put his hands, the girl said, "He barely touched my breast. He was subtle with his approaches and tried to pretend that he was joking, but I was too wary for such as that."

Some workers were unwilling to testify. A tipster pointed out two men, Ely Burdett and James Gresham, who had "informed him that Frank had been familiar with several of the girl employees and that they were afraid to testify against Mr. Frank." Another factory employee seemed conflicted in his testimony when he stated, "I have never seen Mr. Frank do anything unbecoming to a gentleman, except at times when talking to some of the women employees, it seemed to me that he rubbed up against them a little too much."

Former worker Tom Blackstock testified, "I've often seen him picking on different girls," also saying that the superintendent would "rub up against" the girls. This was a phrase that a number of the men who worked in the factory repeated word-for-word. The inquest's jury had to wonder: was this a coincidence, or had they been coached?

Although Leo's testimony made a good impression, the damage to his character was done by the end of the inquest. Thanks to the sensational newspaper coverage, the people of Atlanta viewed him as a

Yankee Jew who had not only forced industrialization upon them and forced their daughters into his factory but who had also attempted to force himself upon those daughters. The inquest's jury came in with these preconceived notions, and it took them only ten minutes to recommend that the police hold Leo Frank, along with Newt Lee, for further questioning in the murder of Mary Phagan.

"HE WASN'T THERE EITHER"

INDICTMENT

Recommending further questioning was one thing. Finding answers that would lead a grand jury to formally charge, or indict, either Leo Frank or Newt Lee for murder was another. Before a suspect could be tried for a crime in a court of law, a grand jury must be presented with enough information to indict him. That job fell to Solicitor General Hugh Dorsey.

As Atlanta's prosecutor, Dorsey's job was to prosecute and convict the accused. Although Dorsey was an ambitious lawyer and politician, he had been remarkably unsuccessful in prosecuting several major cases. He needed a big, public success to bolster his career, and prosecuting the murder of an innocent young girl seemed the perfect opportunity.

Born in a small town, yet raised in the city, Dorsey was capable of acting like a country boy with ordinary working folks or behaving like a shrewdly calculating gentleman in the company of other city lawyers. Dorsey seized authority for the murder case as soon as he could, by ordering the exhumation and autopsy of Mary Phagan himself.

Coroner Paul Donehoo, Dr. Henry Harris, and Fulton County physician J. W. Hurt inspected Mary's body after it was removed from the grave. Dr. Harris paid particular attention to her stomach contents, as this would help him determine the time of death more accurately. Dorsey also ordered the city chemist, Dr. Claude Smith, to test the shirt from Newt Lee's apartment and the bloodstains that Robert Barrett had found in the factory metal shop.

Then Dorsey surprised everyone by ordering a second exhumation of Mary's body two days later and blaming it on police carelessness. Apparently, Dr. Hurt had originally taken hair samples from Mary's body, but they had been lost while in police possession. This time, a fingerprint expert was called in to examine the fingerprints on Mary's throat. Forensic scientists also took photographs of the bite marks on the girl's left shoulder.

Prosecutor Hugh Dorsey in 1913, after the murder of Mary Phagan.

Dorsey quickly began releasing new information to the press. Examining other factory workers than the ones who had testified at the coroner's inquest, he found fourteen-year-old Monteen Stover, who used to work at the factory and still had some pay coming to her. She said she had gone to the pencil factory a little after twelve that Saturday, shortly after the time Mary Phagan would have picked up her pay. "I was sure Mr. Frank would be in his office," Monteen told reporters after speaking with Hugh Dorsey, "so I stepped in. He wasn't in the outer office, so I stepped into the inner one. He wasn't there either. I thought he might have been somewhere around the building, so I waited. When he didn't show up in a few minutes, I went to the door and peered further down the floor among the machinery. I couldn't see him there."

Despite Lemmie Quinn's insistence that Leo had been in his office, Monteen's statement suggested that the superintendent had not been there the whole time. Then Mrs. Nina Formby, a madam of a nearby house of prostitution, claimed that Leo was a regular customer—and that he had called her on Confederate Memorial Day, asking for a place to bring a young girl who'd been taken ill. Mrs. Formby shared her story with the press and even claimed that she was being bribed to keep quiet or leave town until the trial was over.

More evidence poured in. Dorsey's handwriting expert stated that the murder notes could not have been written by Newt Lee.

THE ATLANTA CONSTITUTION

VOL. XLV.—No. 327.   ATLANTA, GA., FRIDAY MORNING, MAY 9, 1913.—FOURTEEN PAGES.   Single Copies on the street, trains and at newsstands, 5 cents. Daily and Sunday, delivered by carrier, by the week, 12 cents.

TARIFF REVISION THROUGH HOUSE; NOW UP TO SENATE

Underwood Measure, Redeeming Party's Platform Pledge, Receives Great Majority.

BATTLE IN THE SENATE PROMISES TO BE BITTER

Republican Senators, However, Admit Measure Will Go Through Practically in the Same Form.

Washington, May 9.—The Underwood tariff bill, proclaimed by the democratic party as the answer to its platform pledge to revise the tariff downward, was passed by the house late today. The vote was 281 to 139, five cross voting against the gill and 2 republicans voting for it. Four progressives supported the bill and four democrats opposed it, while the independent progressive joined with the majority party.

When Speaker Clark announced the vote in loud tones that reverberated his satisfaction in the arrival of the day he long had sought, exuberant democratic leaders stuffed democratic forms over the heads of their colleagues in the rear of the chamber, a fairly rage of applause, followed and the gavel fell on the first chapter in the history of President Wilson's extra session of congress.

With the bill, after a months consideration, on its way to the senate, there was a rush of representatives for their homes tonight. In the forms adjournment will be taken three days at a time beginning next week until June 3. In the meantime, the senate finance committee will study the bill while the house ways and means committee arranges to organize committees preparatory to the transaction of business next month.

Republicans and progressives, led impertinently by Representatives Mann and Murdock, protested to the last against the measure, the former tariff all over written, and proclaiming on the democratic avalanche beaten over the ruins of different tariff commission plan.

Few Democrats Opposed.

Republicans who voted for the bill were Cary and Hatfield, of Wisconsin. Democrats who opposed it were Broussard, Dupre, Lazaro and Morgan, of Louisiana, on account of the schedule reducing sugar 25 per cent and sending it to the free list in three years, and G. S. Smith, of New York.

Progressives who voted for the bill were Kelley and Helgeul, of Pennsylvania; Nolan, of California, and Bryan, of Washington. Kent, of California, formerly a republican, but now an independent progressive, also voted for the bill.

Progressive Leader Murdock and thirteen of his progressive followers voted with the minority. Representative Cooper, a progressive, did not vote, but with the last of the consideration of the measure Minority Leader Mann made a bitterly speech on a point of order by Mr. Underwood to rule out provision for a tariff board in the number by Representative Payne, of New York, to recommit the bill. Speaker Clark contained the point of order. Mann appealed from the chair and roll call was taken on Mr. Underwood's motion to table the appeal, the democratic winning 174 to 142. Progressive Leader Murdock also moved to recommit with instructions to provide for a non-partisan tariff commission, but he failed to get a roll call and the Payne motion to recommit—

Continued on Last Page.

Bargains That You Need Not Hunt For

Advertised in The Constitution today, they will not last long. You had better see them early to avoid the disappointing answer of the salesley, "Sorry, but we've sold out."

Women's Beautiful $7.50 Plumed Hats, now $3.95.
Children's Dainty Parasols, 50c.
Suit cases at $1 and up.
23 pounds of Sugar, $1.
Kingan's Sliced Bacon, 35c.
Best Coal, $4 a ton.

WANTED

You'll find these in the classified pages and they are certainly worth reading to those who have what is asked for:

Woman stenographer and typist at good salary.
Woman teacher for pleasant vacation work.
Salesmen on both salary and commission.
Bungalows, $3,000 to $5,000.

FOR SALE
Four Passenger touring car, $350.

SHRINERS LEAVE FOR CONVENTION

All of the Big Party Are Confident That Atlanta Will Be the Next Convention City.

Two hundred Atlanta shriners leave tonight at 10 o'clock over the Seaboard railroad for Dallas, where they are going to capture the shrine convention for the city in 1914.

Two hundred determined men, with a complete knowledge of what a shrine convention means, will boost Atlanta with every branch during their stay in the southwest, and will bring back with them the promise that the year hence, if not sooner of the Mystic Shrine will journey from every nook of the country to be present and make Atlanta's famed hospitality.

Nothing is lacking to get the War convention money, and much of it, at at least a time $75,000 raised in set of the big drawing cards other is the history of the country have become famed for the next convention—the Shine some time convention is a short time.

it's a short time. Forvent Adair has been a prominent attendant at every Shrine convention in the past fourteen years, and knows exactly what such a convention needs. Not a single detail has been overlooked. The raising of money, the contract with the hotels and the thousand and one other items incident to such a convention has been under the leadership, and now at last his plans are complete.

It is true that O. K. Houck is boosting Memphis—our Atlanta has already left Memphis in the background. Memphis raised $90,000 in about four weeks; Atlanta raised $75,000 in one day! And in addition to the enormous poll that Atlanta will have, a number of other cities have signified their intention of pulling for Atlanta for 1914.

Special Train for Shriners.

When the Southern train pulls out tonight a special section, containing several Pullman sleepers, a Pullman dining car and a Pullman tourist car for the Yaarab Temple's crack drum corps, will be attached.

The latter, an independent organization formed by the temple for shrine conventions and ceremonials, will make a great hit in their red coats and white trousers at Dallas. These trusty fellows are among the best expert in their fun in the country, and will find Atlanta's boys to be many ways that die while away.

On the trip to Dallas short side trips will be made at Birmingham, Ala., Meridian, Miss., and Shreveport, La. Yaarab Temple's drum corps will furnish music. Judge John A. Hynds, W. A. Foster and Claude M. Hutcheson, the editor of interest.

The drum band, forty strong, will carry their drums and fatigue suits. These are as follows:

Captain J. D. Beaumont, First Lieutenant H. C. Adelurd, Second Lieutenant E. G. Van der Veer, First Sergeant W. F. Ferguson, Quartermaster H. M. Miller and Patrolmen Albert Akers, C. E. Barber, J. J. Barnes, Jr., W. D. Benson, F. M. Blackstone, George Argard, R. A. Barnett, G. I. Butler, A. Chapman, R. H. Church, Frank Campbell, B. B. Cunningham, J. C. Downare, George Freeman, L. H. Geiger, H. H. Green, J. L. Grice, J. D. Jones, M. E. McGee, M. N. Mixon, T. A. Mixon, B. A. Osborn, Charles H. Quarles, A. B. Rogers, Louis Stahl, E. B. Roemer, G. Peasley, John Purcell, E. T. Tison, E. D. Tompkins, W. A. Upchurch, W. D. Wald, D. W. Woods, J. C. Wright and Cliff Lanbridge.

Shriners who will go independently are: Fred Messer, I. C. Oberdhorf, A. Dickey, W. R. Joyner, H. G. Harnie, J. B. Desbrowy, Fred Patterson, Dr. R. H. Morton, H. B. Nelson, James J. P. Carson, Fred Van der Veer, J. P. Walti, George Beck, James E. Crack and James Kempton.

Twenty-eight trains, the majority of them special, will be run by the Texas and Pacific railway to Dallas for the big convention. The majority of the shriners will go over these trains.

On Thursday, May 15, the majority of the shriners will leave for their homes, and make fully preparing for the biggest convention that will be held in the Gate City in 1914.

ATLANTA LAW SCHOOL IN NATIONAL CONTEST

Students of the Atlanta Law school have accepted the invitation to compete in the national oratorical contest. Leonard J. Grossman, of the senior class, who won the intercollege state championship for Illinois in 1909, was called upon to outline the details of the coming contest, and the first thought was given championship which will be held next spring.

Walter Turner, field secretary of the Intercollegiate Oratorical association, reported that 100 colleges and universities from twenty-five states would compete for the national prize next year. This list includes Georgia, Georgia Tech, Emory, Mercer, State Normal and other colleges throughout the state. Following this report a local organization was effected.

L. J. Grossman was chosen chairman pro tem, and permanent officers were elected later. The junior class to make arrangements for the national contest next year, the election of president ensued on to a spirited contest between R. J. Webb, of the Atlanta, the B., and H. B. Lee Cook, of Atlanta. The vote was a tie and Mr. Close withdrew in favor of Mr. Webb, who was declared elected. The others are glad of an opportunity to test the law in that regard.

There will rarely be one denied that the state kept open on Sunday, and the globe are glad of an opportunity to test the law in that regard.

Against Change of Name.

Tuscaloosa, Ala., May 8.—The Episc

---

200 LIVES ARE LOST WHEN THE REBELS DYNAMITE TRAIN

Soldiers of Huerta Traveling to Relief Are Besieged. Guaymas Are Blown Up. Only 50 Escape Death.

JAPANESE OFFER AID TO MEXICAN REBELS

Four Hundred Well Armed Subjects of Mikado Want to Fight Huerta—Offer of Japs Refused by Rebels.

WASHINGTON IS UNJUST, SAYS PRESIDENT HUERTA

Mexico City, May 8.—Culminate against Mexico need export as sentiment so long as the Mexican government withholds recognition of the republic. While practically all pending claims have been accepted or arbitrate, they will remain in state plus.

President Huerta called American Ambassador Wilson to the palace today and, after expressing personal and official resentment at the attitude of the administration at Washington, made this declaration. He drew attention to the accomplished and prospective recognition by other nations, and said his attitude was the only one compatible with public opinion and national dignity.

President Huerta declared that a loan had been practically arranged, that the nation was solvent and that Washington was unjust.

Nogales, Ariz., May 8.—Two hundred lives are reported lost in the train disaster at Don, near the Sinaloa-Sonora border.

State troop leaders declare the train bearing 250 federal soldiers was so dynamited by attacks. It is said the insurgents fired into the train, exploding a car of dynamite which the federals were conveying to Guaymas. Only fifty of the passengers are reported to have escaped death and others were wounded. The troops were moving from San Blas, in northern Sinaloa to Alamos below Guaymas, from which point the insurgents feared they could proceed to reinforce the garrison defending the port.

Rebels Surround Parral.

El Paso, Tex., May 8.—Americans arrived here today report that Parral, foreign mining center of southern Chihuahua state, is surrounded by nearly 2,000 constitutionalists and that skirmishes with the federal outposts under radio.

Parral is defended by more than 1,000 men and several minute artillery. The insurgents expect to force surrender when the thirty cars food supply of the town is exhausted.

Another strong force of insurgents is reported moving from the southern part of the state against Chihuahua City, the state capital. The Mexican Central Railway has been destroyed far to the south, preventing the arrival of the federal column, reported moving north from Torreon.

Wilson Watching State Events.

Washington, May 8.—Indications came from the white house today that President Wilson was carefully watching the course of events in Mexico and that the United States government at present was waiting to see if the announced program of the Huerta government to hold loans this provisional election would materialize before deciding the question of recognition. Administration officials say the United States faces the fact although with the defacto government only on business of the most routine character and that it also has had no dealings with the constitutionalists in the north.

MACON CLUBS INDICTED.

Charged With Running "Tippling Houses" on Sunday.

Macon, Ga., May 8.—(Special.)—Grand juries in session here today have returned bills charging several clubs with keeping "tippling houses" open on Sunday. The charges were indicted that the club operated a "blind tiger" on Sunday. All operate open house freely, the officials say, but members do not deny the charge. The clubs say they will fight the charges and the questions will go before a jury.

Cells for the Whites.

Bound Over For Phagan Murder

Photo by Francis B. Price, Staff Photographer.
Leo M. Frank, factory superintendent, who, with Newt Lee, the negro night watchman, was held for the grand jury.

Ere Morgan Sailed to Death He Pledged Woodrow Wilson Money and Influence if Needed

New York, May 8.—"When you see Mr. Wilson tell him for me that if ever there should come a time when he thinks any influence or resources that I have can be used for the country, they are wholly at his disposal."

These, the last words of J. Pierpont Morgan spoken to Colonel George Harvey, the day before Mr. Morgan sailed for Europe, never to return alive, were related tonight to an address by Colonel Harvey before a gathering of bankers and other representative men at a dinner of the trust companies of America. Mr. Morgan was a republican and, in the words of Colonel Harvey, not only regarded his political views with disapproval of Mr. Wilson, with intense apprehension, but never considered the democratic party fully capable of governing this nation. His message to the president, Colonel Harvey, cited as proof of his patriotism.

The Message to Wilson.

"And rising with difficulty from his chair, for he was then quite feeble, he said, with the emphasis that only epidemic thus far.

"When you see Mr. Wilson tell him for me that if there should ever come a time when he thinks any influence or resources that I have can be used for the country, they are wholly at his disposal.

"Barring the usual leave taking, these were the last words I heard from the lips of Mr. Morgan. They were the words of a true patriot, of a great, a very great American, spoken from the depths of a passionately loyal heart. Surely I can do no better than to leave them with you to remember, to cherish and to feel of those on all small live in this, our native land."

Referring to Mr. Morgan's testimony before the Pujo committee at Washington, Colonel Harvey said:

"Although mentally as strong as ever, physically he was sadly broken when summoned to Washington, A his age was then in declining, it was the inevitable ordeal of his life; but it was the end but he had the strength to realize.

"I based to go," he said to me, with characteristic simplicity the day before, 'he said money. I bank to go, but I am glad I went. I think I did myself good.'

"It was a comprehensive utterance in his usual few words—a revelation, too, of his innermost thoughts and conviction. I had spoken of the favorable impression that had been created by his testimony; he had evinced the keenest appreciation.

"'I,' he had said, 'I am convinced that what you say is true. I think they know me better now. I hope they do.

"No sensitive man, no human man or had Mr. Morgan was more sensitive and most human—could have failed to be influenced by the multitude of friendly expressions which had come to him from all sections of the country."

Campaign Episode.

Then followed this curious episode, doubtful curving those hustling on upon on Mr. Morgan said: 'no rise or speak—and a few minutes' silence would come from his eyes than with old determination.

"'And do you recall,' he asked, 'those lines from Scott that you quoted when out man—I was here; now the emphasize upon those two words—when that man had left the room?'

"'Breathes there a man with soul so dead,

"'Who never to himself hath said—' I asked. He nodded and then I continued:

"'This is my own, my native land,' upon which there came from the big gray eyes, so often swimming with old determination, tears to the verge of tears, the eyes of emotion. His voice quivering, he said:

"'That is real patriotism.' And it could recall the remaining lines:

'to do in church, he repeated, as if soliloquizing:

"'Who never to himself hath said, This is my own, my native land.'

The Message to Wilson.

FRANK AND LEE ORDERED HELD BY CORONER'S JURY FOR MARY PHAGAN MURDER

Sensational Statements Made at Inquest by Two Women, One of Whom Had Been an Employee, Who Declared That Frank Had Been Guilty of Improper Conduct Toward His Feminine Employees and Had Made Proposals to Them in the Factory.

EVIDENCE IN BAFFLING MYSTERY THUS FAR, IS CIRCUMSTANTIAL, IS ADMISSION MADE BY DETECTIVES

Frank and Lee Both Go on Stand Again and Are Closely Questioned in Regard to New Lines of Evidence and Forced to Reiterate Testimony Formerly Made to Coroner's Jury. They Will Remain in Jail Pending Action of the Grand Jury.

Leo M. Frank, superintendent of the National Pencil factory, and Newt Lee, the negro night watchman, suspects in the Mary Phagan murder, were ordered by the coroner's jury to be held under charges of murder for further investigation by the Fulton grand jury.

With this verdict the inquest closed at 6:28 o'clock yesterday afternoon. Frank and the negro will be held in the Tower until action is taken by the grand jury and solicitor general. The decision was reached within twenty minutes after the jury had retired.

Although much important testimony was delivered at the inquest, probably the most significant was the admission made by Detective Harry Scott, of the Pinkertons, and Detective John Black, of headquarters, both of whom declared in answer to questions that they so far had obtained no conclusive evidence or clues in the baffling mystery, and that their only success had been attained in the forging of a chain of circumstantial evidence.

Testimony was drawn from a number of women and young girls who told of alleged undue familiarity of the suspected factory superintendent with these and other female employees of the plant. The boldest statement of this character was made by Nellie Pettis, a young sister-in-law of Mrs. Lillie Mae Pettis, an employee of the factory.

She declared that on one occasion, four weeks ago, when she had gone to Frank's office to obtain her sister's pay envelope, the superintendent had made an open proposal, and had even intimated the offer of money.

Frank and Lee on Rack.

Both the superintendent and the negro suspect were placed on the rack during the afternoon session. Lee's statement was a reiteration of his former story. He was questioned on new lines, however, answering all questions promptly and clearly. He preceded his employer.

Frank was interrogated in regard to new evidence that has been obtained by the sleuths.

He was worn and haggard, and shows the effect of his imprisonment. From 9:30 in the morning, at which hour the inquest was resumed, until 5 o'clock in the afternoon, when he was placed on the stand, he sat in the office of Chief Beavers, the object of

---

MRS. WILSON TO NAME POSTMASTER AT ROME

Bowie Will Get Place—Lee Favored Vandiver—Georgia Congressman Alarmed.

By John Corrigan, Jr.

Washington, May 8—(Special.)—Mrs. Woodrow Wilson is to name the postmaster at Rome. She will recommend to the president J. P. Bowie, a friend of her family, and he will receive the appointment.

This information was conveyed to representatives Gordon Lee today after he called at the white house, and he gracefully yielded the place.

Lee Wanted Vandiver.

Mr. Lee was preparing to send on the name of John M. Vandiver, his collector at Rome, for postmaster as postmaster, but the letter found that Mrs. Wilson desired a personal friend whom she had known in better girlhood to be named at Rome. Mr. Vandiver had sought the appointment for more than a year and had the backing of the multitude of friends and organizations which had come to him from all sections of the country.

Mr. Bowie, the choice of Mrs. Wilson is a retired manufacturer of Rome. It has been rumored for several weeks that he would get the place. No opposition could be made against Mr. Bowie, for he is regarded as a man of high character and the selection will meet the approval of the citizens of Rome generally.

Some Hidden Influence.

Following closely upon the rejection of Representative Bell's nominee for the postmastership at Gainesville, this second disappointment of a Georgia representative, has aroused concern among the members of the delegation. None is willing to talk, but all believe some hidden influence is at work to overturn and defeat their plans by any influence felt.

There is more under the surface than has yet come out. When asked about the matter today, Mr. Lee made no comment further than that he could not account for Mrs. Wilson's wishes.

The Gainesville Matter.

There are no new developments in the Gainesville postoffice fight. Representative Bell has not gone prepared the nomination of Mrs. H. C. Ham, whose name was sent by the senate, but has been withheld at the instance of S. E. Hardy to authorities. Until he hears from this his hands will not make any statement.

Senator Hoke Smith called at the white house today and said talk to the president in behalf of Mr. Ham.

POSTMASTER BAKER TO BE INVESTIGATED

Charges Filed at Washington Against Moral Character of Savannah Official.

By John Corrigan, Jr.

Washington, May 8.—(Special.)—Charges against the moral character and fitness for office of Barnes Baker, Jr., postmaster at Savannah, were today filed with the postoffice department by W. G. Cooper, who is under the command of the something

This supported Dorsey's contention that Leo had committed the crime and the night watchman had done nothing except discover the body. Dorsey believed that Leo had often used his status as factory superintendent to get his way with his young female employees and that things had gone wrong with Mary Phagan, leading to violence. However, the evidence that lawyers are allowed to introduce is limited by rules of procedure. Dorsey knew these rules would prevent him from introducing the idea of sexual misconduct, unless the defense first introduced the issue of the superintendent's character. So he decided to force Leo's attorneys to defend their client's character by letting the press run with the rumors about Leo's promiscuous activities. Meanwhile, Dorsey focused on a timeline of circumstantial evidence that would put Leo out of his office and unaccounted for at the time when Mary was killed.

On May 23, 1913, Dorsey convinced the grand jury to indict Leo Frank for the murder of Mary Phagan. He did so without revealing that he had an eyewitness who would be able to describe exactly where Leo was when Mary was killed and how the body ended up in the factory basement.

"WE WANTED ANOTHER STATEMENT"

THE FIRST EYEWITNESS

Dorsey's eyewitness was Jim Conley. Conley, twenty-seven, was a sweeper and odd-jobs man at the factory. He had a drinking problem and lived with a woman he had never married. He was also black. In the eyes of the white Atlanta society of 1913, Conley should have been a prime suspect. He had been in trouble with the law before and had paid several fines and served two sentences on the chain gang, once for attempted armed robbery. But Dorsey, as well as the police, wanted someone other than an African American working man to be guilty of the death of a white girl who had been murdered in a factory. They wanted to convict a white man—and a Yankee industrialist—of this horrendous crime.

Jim Conley from 1914, after the murder of Mary Phagan.

Police had originally questioned Jim Conley about Mary Phagan's death on May 1. He had been seen rinsing out a stained shirt at the factory but had claimed he was trying to wash out rust stains. Police had never tested the shirt for blood because Conley also said he'd been drunk all day Saturday, when Mary was killed, and hadn't been near the factory. And he claimed he couldn't read or write, which meant he couldn't have written the two notes found by Mary's body.

Then Pinkerton agents discovered that witnesses had seen a black man lurking around the factory lobby on Saturday. Detective Black and Pinkerton detective Scott found Jim Conley's signatures on several papers. They compared them with the murder notes and believed the handwriting to be the same. Apparently the man could write. They brought him in again for questioning.

Confronted with his signatures, Conley admitted that he could write but insisted that he had nothing to do with the murder notes. The detectives decided to lock him in an isolation cell to let him think about it. There is no police record showing what Black and Scott said to him, but on May 24, Conley was ready to make a new statement to the police, the Pinkerton investigators, and Hugh Dorsey. It was a completely different statement—one that implicated Leo Frank.

Jim Conley claimed that on Friday, April 25, Frank "asked me could I write and I told him yes I could write a little bit." Then Conley said the superintendent had dictated the two letters that had been found near Mary's body and had given Conley a box of cigarettes and $2.50. Conley stated, "He told me he had some wealthy people in Brooklyn and then he held his head up and looking out of the corner of his eyes said, 'Why should I hang?'"

Initially, the investigators were confused by Conley's statement, because it suggested that Leo had planned the murder the day before and had prepared the notes in advance. Yet Dorsey was convinced it had been a crime of passion. And if Conley *was* speaking the truth, why had he waited so long to come forward? Pinkerton detective Scott later said, "We pointed out to him why the first statement would not fit. We told him we wanted another statement."

Several days later, Conley asked to speak with Detective Black. This time he admitted that he'd made several mistakes the first time. "I made this statement in regard to Friday, in order that I might not be accused of knowing anything of this murder, for I thought that if I put myself there on Saturday, they might accuse me of having a hand in it," he explained. Then he went on to say that on Saturday the superintendent had asked him to sit by the entrance steps until Conley heard him whistle. When he heard the summons, Conley went up to Frank's office and found his boss very nervous and upset. Conley said he then wrote the notes at Leo's dictation, not knowing anything about the murder, and had received the cigarettes and money, as he'd said before.

This second affidavit was more useful to the prosecution, because it confirmed much of their theory of Leo's actions on Saturday. However, the press quickly pointed out that Conley's shifting story implicated himself. Many thought he should be indicted instead of Leo Frank.

The authorities wished that Conley's statement pinned the murder more clearly on Leo's shoulders, so police interrogated the man one more time. Dorsey wasn't present, but his assistant raced back and forth, bringing new questions for the sweeper and carrying his answers back to the solicitor general. This time Conley's affidavit was what the prosecution needed. He combined his previous stories with new details:

> When he whistled for me I went upstairs and he asked
> me if I wanted to make some money right quick and I
> told him "Yes, sir," and he told me that he had picked up
> a girl back there and had let her fall and that her head
> hit against something, he didn't know what it was, and
> for me to move her, and I hollered and told him the girl
> was dead, and he told me to pick her up and bring her to
> the elevator.

Then he described how he had tried to carry the girl, but she proved too heavy for him to manage alone, so the superintendent had helped him carry her onto the elevator and then down to the basement.

After Conley wrote the notes from dictation,

> *Mr. Frank looked at it and said it was all right and Mr.*
> *Frank looked up at the top of the house and said, "Why*
> *should I hang, I have wealthy people in Brooklyn," and*
> *I asked him what about me, and he told me that was all*
> *right about me, for me to keep my mouth shut and he*
> *would make everything all right, and then I asked him*
> *where was the money he said he was going to give me and*
> *Mr. Frank said, "Here is two hundred dollars," and he*
> *handed me a big roll of greenback money.*

Later, Conley added that the superintendent had asked for the money back and said he would give it back on Monday if nothing happened.

This was what Dorsey had been looking for: eyewitness testimony that proved Leo Frank's guilt. The police took Conley to the factory, sent most of the workers home, and had him show them and a group of reporters where all the action of his affidavit had occurred. Repeating his story, Conley led them through the factory, acting out the events as he described them. One of the employees who remained, the day watchman J. M. Holloway, pointed out that the police often corrected Conley. If he said the body was in one place, at times they reminded him it was in a different location:

> *The negro said "let's go back this way", and he shows*
> *them a place about 20 feet the other way, and Lanford*
> *said "Here is where they dropped it". Now they said*
> *"aint this about where you dropped the girl"? and the*
> *negro, he started in another direction, and then he said*
> *"yes sir". They said "aint this where you dropped it"? and*
> *he said "yes".*

But the next editions of the newspapers all praised Jim Conley for coming forward and presented his evidence as absolute truth.

Conley continued introducing new details to flesh out his story for the reporters who crowded around his jail cell. Dorsey was pleased to have his witness, but he was afraid that Conley would say something to contradict his latest statement (which already contradicted his two earlier statements) and damage the case against Leo Frank.

Then the *Georgian* announced that an unnamed man had been shooting craps with Conley in the pencil factory basement on April 26 and had seen Jim Conley himself attack Mary Phagan. The *Georgian* would subsequently identify this witness as Will Green, an African American carnival worker. "This fellow was half drunk and was losing money to me. He got mad and cursed his luck," said Green.

Before long a little girl went upstairs. This negro said he was going to take her money away from her when she came down. I thought he was fooling at first, but when she came down he started for her. I yelled at him not to do it, but he kept right on. Then I skipped out, for I didn't want to get mixed up in any trouble. I stayed around town until the next Monday, and then I read all about how a little girl had been killed . . . and I knew that she was the one I had seen come downstairs at the factory.

A photograph of attorney William Smith after Leo Frank's trial. A newspaper paid Smith to be Jim Conley's lawyer.

Investigators were unable to find the carnival worker and bring him to Atlanta. This was good news for Hugh Dorsey, as it could have damaged his case. He didn't want Conley attracting any more press attention. He met with Chief Lanford and William Smith, Conley's attorney. (Smith was being paid by the *Atlanta Georgian* to represent Jim Conley and to give the paper the inside scoop.) They all agreed that it would be a good idea to return Conley to the police station until the trial, where reporters—and other lawyers—could only speak to him with Smith's or Lanford's approval.

Leo's attorneys, however, worked to stir up public opinion to bring pressure on the State of Georgia to ask the grand jury to indict Jim Conley for Mary's murder. Dorsey resisted strongly, insisting that they had already indicted one man for the crime and should wait until his trial was over before considering any other indictments. In the end, he allowed the grand jury to hear charges against Conley, but Dorsey spoke persuasively to them for an hour, expressing his confidence in his case against Leo Frank and explaining why Conley's indictment would jeopardize it. The grand jury voted almost immediately not to indict Conley.

That left Dorsey free to construct the rest of his case against Leo Frank.

"MOST ALL A PACK OF LIES"

WITNESS PREPARATION

Even before the trial began, George Epps felt a little concerned. There was something about his testimony that the newsboy wanted to discuss with Hugh Dorsey. But George would later say that Dorsey didn't want to hear him, snapping, "Just stick to that." He understood that the solicitor general wanted him to simply repeat his testimony from the inquest, even if he was uncomfortable with some part of it.

George wasn't the only person who got a glimpse of Dorsey's darker side during the days before the trial. The solicitor general summoned numerous potential witnesses to his office, ordering them to be arrested if they did not come willingly. He intended to use not only Leo Frank's teenage employees to prove his case but also anyone who was close to Leo's family.

One of those people was Minola McKnight, the cook in the house Leo and Lucille Frank shared with Lucille's parents, the Seligs. Dorsey needed her testimony to support the timeline he was carefully constructing, a timeline that would leave enough time for Leo to have committed the murder before meeting his father-in-law for lunch. To do that, he wanted to prove that Leo had actually arrived home later than he claimed.

Hearing about the rewards offered by the newspapers, Albert McKnight had told his boss that his wife had information that could help the prosecution, and his boss passed the tip on to the police. But when they questioned Minola, she told them the same story that Leo had told, that he had arrived home at 1:20 and had lunch with his father-in-law because the two ladies had already eaten and were on their way to an opera matinee.

That wasn't what Dorsey hoped to hear. The police called in her husband to "remind" her, but Minola McKnight wouldn't change her story. She even claimed that she and Albert had recently quarreled and suggested that he was lying to get back at her. So the police locked Minola in jail overnight and began grilling the hysterical woman again the following morning. Dorsey probably could not have gotten away with handling most witnesses this way, even a working-class woman, but Minola McKnight was African American. He had no problem ignoring her rights with impunity.

Desperate to be released, she finally signed a statement that said Leo had gotten home at 1:20 but had rushed out again without eating and when he came home that evening, he drank heavily and was too upset to sleep. He told his wife, who then told Minola, that "he was in trouble, that he didn't know the reason why he would murder, and he told his wife to get his pistol and let him kill himself." The statement also said that her employers had started paying her extra after hearing that the solicitor general wanted to question her. "They just said, 'Here is $5, Minola,' but of course I understood what they meant even if they didn't tell me anything . . . I understood it was a tip for me to keep quiet."

After Minola signed this statement, the police released her. Chief Lanford proudly told the press about their new evidence against Leo Frank. But when a reporter from the *Georgian* questioned her about her statement, Minola McKnight told him bitterly, "It's most all a pack of lies."

Furious at the way her family's employee had been treated, Lucille expressed her outrage publicly even though Leo's attorneys urged her to remain silent. She wrote an open letter to Atlanta's citizens that was published in the three main newspapers:

> *That the Solicitor, sworn to maintain the law, should*
> *thus falsely arrest one against whom he has no charge*
> *and whom he does not even suspect and torture her,*
> *contrary to the laws, to force her to give evidence tending*

to swear away the life of an innocent man, is beyond belief.

Where will this end? My husband and my family and myself are the innocent sufferers now, but who will be the next to suffer? . . .

This torturing process can be used to produce testimony to be published in the newspapers to prejudice the case of anyone the Solicitor sees fit to accuse.

Dorsey sidestepped the charges, pointing out "the wife of a man accused of crime would probably be the last person to learn all of the facts establishing his guilt, and certainly would be the last person to admit his culpability," and saying it was his duty to find evidence that would convict someone who had been indicted by the grand jury.

The solicitor general also distracted attention from his misconduct by attacking the police for leaking Minola's affidavit in the first place and threatening to ask the grand jury to investigate the police department. Wanting to avoid such an inspection, Chief Lanford ordered his men to stop sharing details of the case with the press.

Dorsey got the testimony he wanted from some witnesses by simply offering a willing ear. This tactic appealed particularly to the factory girls, who were excited at the idea that all of Atlanta would listen to them. It also worked with some of the factory boys. Another witness told Dorsey that sixteen-year-old Willie Turner had seen Leo Frank and Mary Phagan having a conversation together that suggested the man was making advances and the girl was afraid of him.

Although Willie believed that the girl and his boss had run into each other accidentally, Dorsey repeatedly had him act out the encounter to emphasize that Mary backed away from the superintendent. He tried to persuade the boy to testify that Leo Frank's hands were extended, as if he were trying to grab Mary, although Willie would only go so far in this direction.

When Dorsey couldn't persuade witnesses to testify the way he wanted, he was not above bribing or coercing them. Sixteen-year-old Dewey Hewell, who had worked at the pencil factory, experienced both. Dorsey tracked her down at the Home of the Good Shepherd in Cincinnati, Ohio, a group home for unwed mothers where Dewey was in custody. Dorsey contacted Police Matron Mary Bohnefield and informed her that he believed Dewey could testify about Leo's interest in Mary. Dewey later stated in a sworn deposition that she had been afraid of Bohnefield "and that she was afraid to refuse to testify exactly the way the Police Matron wanted her to." She said that she was promised that she would be released from the group home if she testified against Leo.

At the same time Dorsey was preparing his witnesses, Leo's lawyers were preparing their defense. Reuben Arnold had joined the team of Luther Rosser and Herbert Haas. An expert in evaluating medical evidence and a smooth talker with an encyclopedic knowledge of the law, Arnold balanced Rosser's vigorous oratory style. The first thing the legal team did was instruct Leo to keep silent. They didn't want him giving interviews—perhaps because he was so cool and detail-oriented and that attitude hadn't made a good impression on reporters or perhaps because they simply wanted to keep their strategy to themselves. Either way, the press didn't like it. Reporters took to calling Leo "the silent man in the Tower," referring to his cell in the tower of the station house.

Arnold's and Rosser's strategy was to prove Leo's innocence by convincing the jury that Jim Conley

Attorney Reuben Arnold during Leo Frank's trial in 1913.

was solely responsible for the murder and to undercut all claims of sexual interest in Mary by presenting Conley's motive as greed. They intended to argue that Conley tried to take the money from her pay envelope and when she resisted, he killed her for it. The attorneys found witnesses of their own at the factory to support this contention. Mary Pirk, forelady in the polishing department, told them, "[Jim Conley] borrowed money from me every week. Sometimes he wouldn't pay me, and I would come in the office and get it."

Other factory girls would confirm Mary Pirk's testimony about Conley's habit of borrowing money from them. They also said that he behaved strangely on the Monday after the murder. And police had never found Mary's silver mesh purse, further evidence that her murder had been the result of robbery gone bad.

The defense also had a witness who claimed that Jim Conley had confessed to the murder. William Mincey was an insurance agent for American Life. He was also a white man, so the attorneys were confident that his race would make him believable, especially to the all-white jury they expected to get. After watching the Confederate Memorial Day parade, Mincey had gone back to selling insurance door to door. He'd seen a man who identified himself as Jim Conley and tried to sell the man some insurance, but Conley was nervous and almost incoherent. He told Mincey to come back the following week, but when Mincey pressed him, Conley said he was in trouble and expected to be in jail soon. The insurance agent asked what for, and Conley replied, "Murder, I killed a girl today."

Mincey asked why, and Conley got angry. "That is for me to know and you to find out," he snapped. Mincey tried to get more information and started to come closer, offering to write the man's insurance application right then. But Conley jumped up and backed away, saying, "I have killed one today and I don't want to kill another."

When he read about Mary's murder, Mincey went to the factory, but things were so hectic that day watchman Holloway turned him away. Mincey said he'd gone to the police station right after Conley had been arrested and been allowed to see him, but Conley claimed he didn't remember Mincey or the conversation. Then Mincey wrote to Dorsey about the meeting but never got a reply, so he contacted Rosser. The defense team found several women who had heard the men's conversation on Confederate Memorial Day and agreed to testify.

Leo's attorneys also planned to use medical experts to show that Mary Phagan could well have been killed later than Dorsey claimed, while Leo was outside the factory building. At this point, Arnold and Rosser felt well prepared to go to trial. They believed that all Dorsey had was a distorted timeline and an eyewitness who was lying to protect himself. The defense was confident that a jury would compare the compelling evidence against Jim Conley with the weak circumstantial case against Leo and quickly declare him not guilty.

"ISN'T THIS A LARK?"

THE TRIAL OPENS

As July 1913 drew to a close, many of the teenage factory employees were in a state of thrilled anxiety. Would Hugh Dorsey call them to the stand? Would all of Atlanta hear what they could tell?

Temperatures topped one hundred degrees daily that July, and it looked as if heat might postpone the trial still longer. (Air conditioners were not yet used widely.) But Judge Leonard Roan wanted to proceed. Normally the trial would have been held in the Thrower Building because the new county courthouse was still under construction. But authorities anticipated large crowds for this trial. So they created a courtroom that would seat about 250 people out of a big room on the first floor of the old city hall. They installed fans and extra chairs beneath the electric chandeliers hanging from the tin ceiling and also a ventilating device called an ozonator. Unfortunately, the ozonator didn't cool the room very well, so Judge Roan ordered the windows opened to bring in fresh air.

The open windows also brought the overflow crowd that had gathered in the streets into the room. And while the judge could control the behavior of the people seated in his packed courtroom, he could do nothing about the crowd outside. People cheered, booed, and shouted at the witnesses, the lawyers, the judge, and even the jury. They threatened, "Hang that Jew, or we'll hang you!" Although the defense protested, Judge Roan simply asked the sheriff to find out who was making the noise. That did nothing to stop the crowd's commentary on the proceedings.

Passions ran high in the courtroom as well. A Georgia general assemblyman who attended part of the trial recalled, "There was a thirst for the blood of Mary Phagan's murderer. So intense was this feeling that the very atmosphere in and about the courthouse was charged with the sulphurous fumes of anger. I was in the courthouse several times during the trial, and the spirit, the feeling, the thought of the crowd affected me. Without reason, I found myself prejudiced against Frank. Prejudiced, not from facts and testimony, but by popular belief and hostile feeling manifested by the crowd."

Witnesses waited to testify in an upstairs room above the courtroom. The *Atlanta Journal* reported the crowd could see the factory girls at the open windows, laughing and chattering with one another, "Are you subpoenaed? Isn't this a lark?"

For those in the courtroom, it was anything but a lark. Hugh Dorsey knew he had to win this trial or say good-bye to his ambitions of climbing to higher political position. Judge Roan knew that this high-profile case would demand his careful rulings on the evidence or the verdict might be overturned on appeal. The twelve men on the jury knew from the crowd noise that all of Atlanta would be paying attention to their decision.

Prosecutor Hugh Dorsey (standing) questions Newt Lee (sitting on witness stand). *Left inset:* Judge Leonard S. Roan at the time of Leo Frank's trial. *Right inset:* Leo Frank looks on.

And Leo Frank, sitting at the defense table with his wife and his mother beside him, knew that his attorneys had to prove his innocence or he would lose his life. The penalty for murder in 1913 Georgia was to be hanged by the neck until dead. Despite this terrible prospect, Leo seemed calm and collected as he entered the courtroom.

THE ATLANTA CONSTITUTION

THE STANDARD SOUTHERN NEWSPAPER.

Vol. XLVI.—No. 51. ATLANTA, GA., WEDNESDAY MORNING, AUGUST 6, 1913. —TWENTY PAGES. Daily and Sunday, carrier delivery, 12 cents weekly. Single copies on the streets and at newsstands, 5 cents.

CONLEY'S MAIN STORY STILL REMAINS UNSHAKEN

MOTHER AND SON MEET DEATH WHEN TRAIN HITS AUTO

Mrs. Emma Heard and Lindon Heard, 10 Years Old, of Vienna, Killed Near McDonough on Way to Motordrome Races.

HEARD ESCAPES DEATH BY LEAP FROM MACHINE

Both Automobile and Southern Train Were Traveling at Rate of About 25 Miles an Hour—Car Stopped on Tracks.

Mrs. Emma Heard, age 31, of Vienna, wife of J. P. Heard, Jr., son of the late Senator Heard, and her son, Lindon Heard, age 10 years, were struck and instantly killed by a train Tuesday afternoon about 2 o'clock, while crossing the Southern railway tracks one mile north of McDonough, Ga.

Mrs. Heard, with her husband and son, was en route to Atlanta, from Vienna, to attend the races at the Motordrome Tuesday night, when the accident occurred. The scene of the tragedy is located about a mile from McDonough. At this point a train cannot be seen from the road until the driver of a vehicle is near the tracks.

Mr. Heard Driving Car.

Mr. Heard, who was driving the car, which was a two-passenger roadster, was seated on the opposite side of the car from the approaching train, and was driving down the hill leading to the tracks at a speed of twenty-five miles an hour.

Mrs. Heard, on the other seat, first sighted the train, when the automobile was within ten yards of the track. She shouted to Mr. Heard that a train was coming and he immediately applied the emergency brake. The brake for some reason failed to perform its proper function and the car rolled on, coming to a dead stop directly in the path of the train. Seeing all hope of getting the car from the track was gone, Mr. Heard leaped out of the car, at the same time shouting, "For God's sake, jump."

His wife and son, however, were too late, and the train struck the automobile directly in the middle, going at the rate of thirty miles per hour. Mrs. Heard was caught on the front of the engine and dragged a distance of 16 feet, while her son was trailed alongside the engine for 50 feet.

The train was stopped, but when passengers reached the side of Mrs. Heard and her son, it was found that the lives of both were already extinct.

Story Told by Father.

Mr. Heard, nearly prostrated with grief, incoherently told the story of the accident, as follows:

"Mrs. Heard, my son Lindon and myself left our home in Vienna this morning for Atlanta, where we were going to attend the motorcycle races. We were in my car, which was a small two-passenger roadster. We left Indian Springs, where we lunched, about 1 o'clock, and it must have been just a little after 2 when we passed through McDonough.

"Not more than 10 minutes later we passed over the brow of a long, steep hill, which leads down to the railroad tracks. A train cannot be seen until one is almost on the crossing. We were only a few yards from the track when my wife shouted that there was a train approaching. I was driving at the rate of 20 or 25 miles an hour. I shut off the engine at once, and applied the brake. It failed to work, and the car ran directly on the track. Seeing that we would be struck I jumped from the car and shouted for my wife and son to do likewise. They were probably too frightened to do so, and a few seconds after I jumped the car was struck. I do not remember what happened after that."

The bodies of the victims were brought to Atlanta Tuesday afternoon, and taken to Patterson's undertaking establishment for preparation for burial.

Heards Are Well Known.

Mrs. Heard was formerly Miss Emma Lashley, daughter of Mr. and Mrs. J. J. Lashley, and has at all times been prominently identified with all movements for social and civic betterment

Continued on Page Four.

BREAD IS THE STAFF OF LIFE

But no man amounts to anything if he makes existence one big loaf.

It's the workers, not the shirkers, that keep receiving tellers busy making entries in their favor.

Luck's only a name for hard work. There's no limit to the height you can reach—if you'll work.

But if you play you'll have to pay in time and money wasted opportunities and loss of self-respect.

Get busy now. Read The Constitution want ads. Men are calling for you. If you don't find your job there go after it with a Wanted Situations ad.

If it pays others to pay for Constitution want ads it will pay you, too, for—

"You Can't Get Something For Nothi[illegible]

WOMEN ARE PLAYING BIG PART IN TRIAL OF FRANK

From left to right: Striking photograph of Mrs. Leo Frank as she entered the courtroom Tuesday afternoon; grandmother of Mary Phagan. Two women spectators, who were excluded from the trial during Jim Conley's testimony.

Photos by Francis E. Price, Staff Photographer.

BANDITS ROB TRAIN AND PUT HANDCUFFS ON THE MAIL CLERKS

Two White Men Hold Up the Fast Louisville and Nashville No. 4 Near Calera, Alabama.

ALL REGISTERED MAIL TAKEN BY THE ROBBERS

Three Mail Clerks Handcuffed—Robbers Escape as the Train Enters the Suburbs of Birmingham.

Birmingham, Ala., August 5.—The mail car on the fast Louisville and Nashville train No. 4 from New Orleans was robbed early tonight by two unknown white man. All of the registered mail was taken, but no estimate could be made tonight of the amount secured.

The train reached Birmingham on time at 8:37 p. m. and two of the mail clerks, George Hoover and T. G. York, were found handcuffed so that the irons had to be filed from their wrists, while Chief Clerk Harry Everett had his thumbs securely tied together with heavy twine.

The robbers boarded the mail car at Calera, on the dark side, after the train had begun to move. The clerks state that they were immediately covered with pistols and ordered to turn their faces to the wall.

Robbers Leap From Train.

Everett looked around once and was fired upon, the shot striking the corner of the car near his head. The robbers jumped from the train at Fourteenth street in Birmingham.

Chief Clerk Everett says has has no idea how much of value there was in the registered mail, but that the men took it all. He says they were both short, slender men, but they did not get a good look at the robbers' faces, as they were forced to keep their own faces turned to the wall.

The clerks first saw the robbers jump to the mail car on their hands and knees. One robber kept his pistols on the men while the other ransacked the mail. The distance from Calera to Birmingham is 33 miles so that they had plenty of time to make a thorough job. No one else on the train apparently knew that the robbers were aboard.

Handcuffed Men Found.

When the engineer stopped for the Southern crossing at Fourteenth street, Birmingham, he happened to look back and saw the two men jump from the mail car door. This aroused his suspicion and an investigation revealed the handcuffed clerks.

A quick run was then made to the Louisville and Nashville station, where the alarm was given. Every police station was quickly notified and automobiles with detectives started in pursuit.

E. G. York, one of the clerks in the car tonight, was also in the Louisville and Nashville mail car which was [illegible]

LOBBY USED MONEY TO KEEP ITS FOES OUT OF CONGRESS

Chief Counsel Emery Frankly Tells How Manufacturers Fought Congressmen Who Couldn't Be Controlled.

UNDERWOOD INTERVIEW DESCRIBED BY EMERY

Emery Tells How Efforts Were Made to Control Certain Committees—"Democratic Simplicity" Ridiculed

Washington, August 5.—From the files of the National Association of Manufacturers today came the details of legislative activities of the widest range, extending from the home districts of members of congress throughout the country to the white house and the capitol.

While the senate lobby investigators pursued their probe by an examination of former Senator Joseph R. Foraker, of Ohio, the house committee got under way and placed in the recor da hundred letters from the files of James A. Emery, chief counsel for the National Association of Manufacturers.

Wide Range of Activities.

From attempts to influence the selecting of the labor and judiciary committees of the house, the discussions of the possibility of coupling currency legislation with the tariff bill at the present session of congress; from conversation with Majority Leader Oscar Underwood, of the house, to letters and telegrams to Presidents Wilson and Taft, the correspondence covered every field of public policy and legislative practice.

Frankly and quietly, Emery, on the stand, acknowledged that he had recommended a contribution of $500 to oppose Representative Buchanan, of Illinois, for re-election, and told of personal interviews with leaders and members of congress in his attempts to influence the naming of committees or to prevent the enactment of legislation urged by organized labor.

The correspondence suggested a bitter feud between the National Association of Manufacturers and the American Federation of Labor in an attempt to secure control of the legislative agencies of the government.

Knocks for Labor Department.

Discussing the recent sundry civil bill, with its provisions prohibiting the expenditure of certain funds for the prosecution of farmers and labor unions under the Sherman law, Emery wrote to President John Kirby, Jr., of the association, March 7, 1913, after President Taft had vetoed the bill:

"I want to emphasize as hard as I can the importance of lining up for a tremendous demonstration when this bill reaches President Wilson, as it undoubtedly will, with the same provision in it.

"You will then have an early opportunity to decide whether the glittering democratic motto, 'Equal rights for all and special privileges for none,' means anything, or whether the administration has surrendered completely or will merely turn over the department of labor.

"I note your reference to a letter

With Session Near Close Lower House Is Plunged Into All Day Filibuster

With State's Revenues Showing Loss of Over $1,000,000 and Need of Some Action to Relieve Financial Stringency Greater Than Ever, Whole Day Is Wasted by Legislators.

EFFORT MADE TO FORCE COMMITTEE TO REPORT WEBB BILL, THE CAUSE

Wohlwender, of Muscogee, Leads Opposition to Resolution Introduced by Kidd, of Baker, and Is Given Assistance in Fight by Myrick and Shruptrine, of Chatham.

With six more days, exclusive of Saturday and Sunday, in which the legislature may take some action to relieve the financial stringency of the state, ninety-five counties heard from show a total decrease from the revenues of last year of $1,000,000.

Meanwhile, the house is paralyzed by a filibuster which lasted through both the morning and afternoon sessions of Tuesday, and the end of which is not yet in sight.

At 11:45 o'clock Tuesday morning the house was just ready for the special continuing order, which was the automobile registration tax bill, when Mr. Kidd, of Baker, introduced a resolution claiming that the temperance committee had usurped the power of the house when it denied the house the consideration of the Searcy-Hixon (Webb) bill of the senate, which is to enforce in Georgia the provisions of the 'federal act known as the Webb bill regulating the shipment of liquor into 'dry' states. The resolution demanded that the bill be submitted to the house for consideration.

Referred to Subcommittee.

This bill was referred by the temperance committee to a subcommittee which was instructed to look into the constitutionality of the measure and report to the 1914 session of the legislature. The question of the constitutionality of the federal bill is now pending in the United States supreme court.

Mr. Wohlwender, of Muscogee, immediately took the floor to oppose the resolution, declaring that the action of the temperance committee was nothing more than to withhold action on the bill until its constitutionality could be determined.

When Mr. Wohlwender continued to hold the floor, and Messrs. Myrick and Shuptrine, of Chatham, came to his assistance, the house first woke to the realization that it was in the grasp of a filibuster.

The object of the members conduct-

1 DEAD, 2 WOUNDED AS RESULT OF FEUD

G. M. Crawford Killed and Brother and C. W. Cobb Badly Wounded at Moniac, Georgia.

Valdosta, Ga., August 5.—(Special.)—In a deadly hand-to-hand fight at Moniac, Ga., yesterday G. M. Crawford, a prominent citizen of that place, was shot and killed, his brother wounded and C. W. Cobb, of Hazlehurst, Ga., stabbed and cut in more than a dozen places. Cobb was brought to this city today, suffering from sixteen knife wounds, and is receiving medical attention here.

According to the story told by Cobb, he was attacked at Moniac by the four Crawford brothers, and after killing one of them and shooting another, he was cut almost to death. He has severe stabs in the head and was almost disemboweled. He lost consciousness before the fight ended and says that he was left by the Crawfords in the woods where he remained all night and was found senseless Tuesday morning.

A message from Moniac states that the trouble between Cobb and the Crawfords is of long standing, growing out of some real estate transactions. J. M. Crawford met Cobb on his arrival at Moniac yesterday and requested payment of a debt he claimed was due him. The quarrel and shooting followed. Brothers of Crawford are said to have disarmed Cobb and to have cut him.

All of the parties are prominent. Cobb is a real estate dealer at Hazlehurst.

GIRL LOCKED IN CLOSET FOR NEARLY 72 HOURS

Chicago, August 5.—After being locked in the closet of a vacant house for nearly 72 hours, 5-year-old Annie Newman was released from her prison this afternoon so weak from want of food that she may die.

Together with several playmates the child was playing "hide-and-seek" on Saturday afternoon in a vacant house four doors from her home at East Chicago, Ind. She hid in the closet and closed the door which had been recently varnished. She was found today by a real estate agent who was showing prospective buyers through the house. The door had stuck and the child had been unable to open it.

GREEN SOCKS CAUSED DEATH OF SHERWOOD

Birmingham, Ala., August 5.—William A. Sherwood, of Evansville, Ind., died at a local hospital last night from blood poisoning caused by wearing green socks. Sherwood had a slight abrasion on his foot last week and put on a new pair of green silk hose. The foot soon began swelling and he [illegible]

KEEP HANDS OFF, CRIES GEN. HUERTA TO UNITED STATES

Mexican President Announces He Will Not Treat With Ex-Gov. Lind, the Personal Agent of President Wilson.

PROPOSAL TO MEDIATE AN INSULT TO MEXICO

Huerta Declares He Will Resent Any Insult to National Dignity — Implacable War to Be Waged on Rebels.

"KEEP YOUR HANDS OFF," HUERTA TELLS U. S.

Mexico City, August 5.—President Huerta tonight reiterated the declaration of his policy of "hands off" in the reply to a question as to what would be his attitude in case an offer of mediation should be made by the United States through John Lind who is coming here as the personal representative of President Wilson to act as adviser to the American embassy.

"I have said publicly," President Huerta declared, "that I will not accept mediation or intervention of any kind, because national dignity and honor do not exact it. I have declared also that I will not treat with the rebels, and much less will I do so if the insinuation that I do involves a flagrant violation of our sovereignty.

"The question of dignity admits of no transactions and the present struggle should be conducted implacably until the national aspirations are satisfied. All should be joined in the bonds of peace, rejecting all suggestions of a violation of sovereignty and any insult that may be offered to our national dignity."

That any suggestion by Mr. Lind or any other foreigner that President Huerta shall resign in favor of a provisional president, or that a compromise be effected with the rebels, will be regarded as unfriendly interference and resented by the government, was the comment of one man high in official life today. As simply a personal representative of President Wilson, this man continued, Mr. Lind might come to Mexico, but if he attempted to interfere with the politics of the country, he must be ignored.

Unless there is a radical change in sentiment it is not impossible that the reception accorded Mr. Lind will be exciting. Already there is talk of public demonstrations of disapproval at his coming.

Washington, August 5.—With former Governor John Lind, of Minnesota, on his way to Mexico City as the personal representative of President Wilson, the eyes of the administration today were turned expectantly to the capital of the southern republic for the next developments.

Secretary Bryan expects Mr. Lind to be in Mexico City by the end of the

[illegible]d on Page Seven.

GRILLED 12 HOURS BY LUTHER ROSSER JIM CONLEY INSISTS FRANK GUILTY MAN

Declaring That "I Don't Remember," or, "No, Sir; I Didn't Say That," or Simply Affirming Blandly That He Had Lied on a Previous Occasion, Negro Sweeper Sticks to Story Told on the Witness Stand on Monday Morning Despite Most Rigid Cross-Examination of Trial.

AFFIDAVIT BY MINCEY OF CONLEY CONFESSION IS DENIED BY WITNESS

Apparently Despairing of Breaking the Negro, Attorneys for Defense Appeal to Judge Roan to Strike All Evidence Relating to Alleged Previous Conduct of Frank Before Day of Murder on Ground of Irrelevancy — State Vigorously Protests Against Such Action and Judge Roan Will Decide Today.

Twelve and one-half hours under the merciless cross-questioning of Luther Rosser, than whom no lawyer at the Atlanta bar has more terrors for the average witness; twelve and one-half hours saying, "I don't remember," "No, sir, I didn't say 'dat,'" or simply affirming blandly that he had lied on a previous occasion; twelve and one-half hours staring fixedly on a crowded court room; twelve and one-half hours without the solace of a cigarette; twelve and one-half hours during which time the perspiration or sweat—if you like that word better—failed to dot his brow—

That is the record of Jim Conley, former negro sweeper at the National Pencil factory.

No such record has ever been made in a criminal case in this county.

On Monday Conley was on the stand five hours and a half, and the able attorneys for the defense failed to break him down; failed to rattle him. On Tuesday, after a good night's sleep at the Tower, Conley resumed the stand and Luther Rosser questioned him for seven hours. Still he did not shake him.

Conley may be telling the truth in the main or he may be lying altogether. He may be the real murderer or he may have been but the accomplice after the fact. Be these things as they may, he is one of the most remarkable negroes who has ever been seen in this section of the country. His nerve seems unshakable. His wit is ever ready.

Lawyers Work In Vain.

As stated in Tuesday's Constitu-

Weather Prophecy

UNSETTLED.

Georgia — Unsettled Wednesday; Thursday probably fair; light variable winds.

Local Report.

Lowest temperature	74
Highest temperature	92
Mean temperature	83
Normal temperature	77
Rainfall in past 24 hours, inches	.02
Deficiency since 1st of mo., inches	.87
Deficiency since Jan. 1, inches	1.22

Reports From Various Stations.

STATIONS AND State of WEATHER.	Temperature. 7 p.m.	Temperature. High	Rain 24 hr's Inches.
Atlanta, cloudy	83	92	.02
Baltimore, clear	78	82	.00
Birmingham, clear	88	96	.00
Boston, pt. cloudy	70	80	.00
Buffalo, pt. cldy.	70	74	.00
Charleston, cloudy	82	86	.00
Jacksonville, cldy.	78	90	.00
Kansas City, clr.	100	102	.00
Memphis, clear	90	94	.00
Miami, cloudy	82	88	.00
Mobile, clear	86	98	.00
Montgomery, pt. c.	88	98	.00
New Orleans, clr.	90	94	.00
New York, clear	70	78	.00
Oklahoma, clear	94	100	.00
Raleigh, cloudy	68	84	1.28
St. Louis, pt. cldy.	88	90	.00
Sheridan, cloudy	74	78	.04
Tampa, pt. cloudy	82	84	.00
Toledo, pt. cloudy	74	80	.00
Washington, clear	74	84	.00

C. F. von HERRMANN, Section Director.

Much like modern TV news, Georgia newspapers tried to provide constant coverage to a public eager to hear any news of the trial.

"I am glad the trial is about to begin after this long wait," he declared. "I have no fear. I am not only innocent of this crime, but I am innocent of any knowledge of it." For her part, Lucille sat close to her husband and glared steadily at the prosecutor with fury as he opened his case.

Hugh Dorsey put Mary Phagan's mother on the stand first, reminding the jury that Mary had been a pretty, innocent young girl forced to work in a factory. Then he called George Epps, who boyishly leaped to the stand, barefoot. The judge ruled that George couldn't repeat what he claimed Mary told him on the streetcar, but George testified to the time he met Mary and the time he saw her go into the factory. When asked what time he'd finished selling his papers, he said he wasn't sure because he told time by the sun, and the sun had gone down by then.

That statement gave Luther Rosser his cue for cross-examination—it had been a gray, rainy day that Saturday, with no sun. This would be his technique throughout the trial: to trip up witnesses on technical errors, implying their whole evidence was a lie because of those small lies. It was a reasonable strategy, but it was a calculated, rational approach that didn't take into account the passion of the crowd—or the passion of the jury. In contrast, Dorsey understood that the way to a jury's heart was to tell a story they could believe, because a convincing story cannot be refuted by fact. He wove a powerful tale that caught up both the jury and the crowd in its emotion. Rosser tried to make them think about the facts, but it was very difficult to make reason outweigh emotion.

Newt Lee testified about finding the body and notifying the police—and about not being able to reach Leo Frank. He was followed on Tuesday and Wednesday by a string of police witnesses, including Pinkerton detective Scott and culminating in Detective John Black. Black, especially, presented all Leo's actions in as suspicious a light as possible, particularly his unwillingness to help with the investigation or even speak to police without his lawyers present after his arrest.

Leo listened, his impassive expression masking his inner outrage. He knew he'd had good reason not to talk to detectives. "I knew that there would not be an action so trifling, that there was not an action so natural but that they would distort and twist it to be used against me," he later explained, "and that there was not a word that I could utter that they would not deform and distort and use against me."

Detective Black's testimony was specific and detailed under the direct examination by Solicitor General Dorsey, but it dissolved into a repetition of "I don't know" when Luther Rosser took over on cross-examination. This prompted Rosser to demand at one point, "Why is it you recollect so well some things, and fail so badly in others?" Black had no answer.

On Thursday fourteen-year-old Monteen Stover testified that she had come to the factory on April 26 to get her pay and that Leo Frank was not in his office, contradicting Leo's statement that he worked on paperwork after he paid Mary. Rosser was careful in his cross-examination of the girl, getting her to admit that she might not have seen Leo since the open safe door blocked her view. But he didn't want to appear bullying, and his polite questions couldn't shake her insistence that she hadn't paid attention to furniture or doors because she was looking for a person, not an object.

Robert Barrett testified about the hair and blood he had found. Then the chemist, Dr. Claude Smith, testified that the chips of wood from the floor of the metal room were indeed stained with blood, although Rosser got him to admit that he couldn't identify the blood and it "might have come from a mouse."

More medical evidence followed on Friday, with the appearance of Dr. Henry Harris, who had performed the autopsy on Mary Phagan. He testified that the blows to her face looked as if they had been made with a fist and that the condition of the bread and cabbage in her stomach indicated she had been killed only thirty or forty-five minutes after eating. Since Mary had eaten shortly before leaving home, that would put her time of death just after she entered the factory for her pay.

But Dr. Harris's most surprising testimony was still to come. "I made an examination of the privates of Mary Phagan," he explained. "I found no spermatozoa. On the walls of the vagina there was evidence of violence of some kind . . . The dilation of the blood vessels indicated to me that the injury had been made in the vagina some little time before death. Perhaps ten to fifteen minutes."

Dr. Harris had just stated that Mary Phagan appeared to have been raped by some object that did not leave any semen. In so doing, he laid the groundwork for Dorsey's plan to build on this implication to accuse Leo of being a pervert.

But before the defense could cross-examine Dr. Harris, he complained he was too ill to continue, and Judge Roan excused him on the grounds that he would return as soon as he was able. When Dr. Harris did return to complete his testimony, he focused solely on the time of death, and Arnold was unable to shake the doctor's claims during his cross-examination.

Setting up the main case against Leo, the prosecution proceeded to call a witness who had seen Jim Conley in the factory lobby the day Mary was killed. Dorsey ended the day by calling Albert McKnight. Even though his wife, Minola, had retracted her earlier statement, McKnight was still willing to testify in hopes of getting some of the reward money that had as yet gone unpaid. On cross-examination Rosser forced McKnight to reveal some of the details of his wife's mistreatment at the hands of the police, but he couldn't trip the man up on any of his own testimony.

Sixteen-year-old Helen Ferguson eagerly took the stand on Saturday morning, wearing a pretty white dress with a bow at the neck. She testified that she had tried to pick up her close friend Mary's pay from Leo Frank on Friday, but he wouldn't give it to her. Helen told the jury that the superintendent said that Mary would get it on Saturday, implying that he intended to see the girl then.

Dr. Hurt, the Fulton County medical examiner, reinforced Dr. Harris's testimony about the blows to Mary's face but was less convincing about the charge of rape, stating, "I discovered no violence to the [genital] parts." Reuben Arnold handled the cross-examination, getting the doctor to concede that the blood the police noted on her thighs might have simply been the girl's menstrual period.

The trial almost ended at that point. After a break, Judge Roan came back into the courtroom carrying a copy of the *Georgian*. Jurors could clearly see the bright red headline about the case:

THE ATLANTA CONSTITUTION
THE STANDARD SOUTHERN NEWSPAPER

THE STANDARD SOUTHERN NEWSPAPER

Vol. XLVI—No. 66.　　　ATLANTA, GA., THURSDAY MORNING, AUGUST 21, 1913.—FOURTEEN PAGES.　　　Daily and Sunday, carrier delivery, 12 cents weekly. Single copies on the streets and at newsstands, 5 cents.

EVIDENCE ENDED; ARGUMENT WILL OPEN TODAY

HUERTA INFORMS WILSON THAT HE LACKS SUPPORT OF THE AMERICAN PEOPLE

Some Tart Intimations by the Mexican General in His Reply to the Note Delivered by Lind.

HUERTA BLAMES WILSON FOR MEXICAN CIVIL WAR

He Says if Wilson Had Refused Recognition Peace Would Have Been Restored. He Warns Wilson His Power Is Only Temporary.

Washington, August 20.—Intimations are contained in provisional President Huerta's reply to the American note presented by John Lind that President Wilson is not backed up by congress or the American people in his stand against recognition of the Huerta government.

Referring to the attacks on the Washington administration by members of congress and pointing to the official recommendations of Ambassador Henry Lane Wilson against recognition, Huerta declares he is entitled to be recognized. He holds that the democratic party's power is temporary, and argues that recognition of his government is a partisan question in the United States. He states his intimation not to reaches his conclusion on private advices from Washington.

This information was obtained tonight from those who know the contents of the Huerta note so far as it has been deciphered. The complete note is not yet at hand, but the principal argument has been placed before administration officials.

Neither Side Is Receding.

Though negotiations between John Lind, personal representative of President Wilson and Provisional President Huerta are continuing on a cordial personal basis, neither side is receding from its position, and administrative measures already are under contemplation here. No definite course has been formulated, but the policy which can prevent is under consideration, and is most likely to be adopted is one of absolute non-interference.

The American government under such a policy would continue to deny arms to both sides, would withdraw Americans from trouble zones, insist on proper protection to property and lives, and, in effect, let the Mexicans continue their controversy on the battlefield.

The administration is determined against intervention or war, and the other alternative, friendly mediation, apparently has failed. Officials here believe, however, that the United States, through the mission of Mr. Lind, will have satisfied foreign governments generally of the desire to

Continued on Page Nine.

How's Your Office Boy?

Bright youngster, with get-up-and-go? Always busy doing what he should be?

If not, and you know the ratio of an energetic lad in your office, phone a Want ad to Main 5000 or Atlanta 103.

The Constitution will find you the kind of boy you want. In short order, too. Send you a number of applicants from which to take your pick.

First thing every morning people in search of work or better jobs read The Constitution Want Ads.

Index to Want Ads Page 10, Col.2.

"You Can't Get Something for Nothing."

THE ATLANTA CONSTITUTION

BLAMING THE GIRL DIDN'T SAVE DIGGS FROM FEDERAL PEN

He's Found Guilty on Four Counts Out of Six and May Be Sentenced for Twenty Years.

CAMINETTI TO BE TRIED ON A SIMILAR CHARGE

In Summing Up, Diggs' Attorney Didn't Palliate Offense But, Like His Client, Blamed the Girl.

San Francisco, Cal., August 20.—Eloping with Marsha Warrington from Sacramento, Cal., to Reno, Nev., Maury L. Diggs, former state architect of California, was guilty of violating the Mann act, which makes it a felony to transport women for immoral purposes from one state to another. This was the verdict tonight of the jury that tried him.

After using but three hours and five minutes, the jury returned to ask the court what form the verdict should take if they were agreed on some of the counts in the indictment and not on the others.

Judge Van Fleet instructed them to make their findings on those count as to which they were agreed. A verdict of guilty on any one count, he said would be a verdict of guilty of violating the statute, and would carry with it the penalty imposed by the statute.

Diggs May Get 20 Years.

There were six counts in the indictment, and the jury found a verdict of guilty on the first four. Each count carries a maximum penalty of five years and a minimum of one year in a federal penitentiary.

Diggs, his wife, father, mother and his three aunts, Mrs. Dease Cambridge and Mrs. Anthony Caminetti, were in court, waiting for the verdict. Diggs was pale, and his wife showed the fatigue she was under by the twitching of her lips, and the incessant bloom of her rich color.

The questions of the foreman plainly foreshadowed the coming verdict and gave them time to steel themselves for the final shock. There was no change

Continued on Page Nine.

CARDS ARE STACKED TO PUT HARRY THAW ON AMERICAN SOIL

Canadian Immigration Authorities Plan to Drop Stanford White's Slayer In Vermont Sometime Tonight.

IMMIGRATION BUREAU SUPERIOR TO COURTS

If Thaw Wins in Court Inspectors Propose to Seize Him and Rush Him Over Border—Thaw Worried.

"GIVE HIM A CHANCE!" SHOUT THE CANADIANS

Sherbrooke, August 20.—Sentiment in Sherbrooke is distinctly in Harry Thaw's favor. A crowd which greeted him at the station when he arrived from Coaticook shouting:

"Let him go! Set him free! He hasn't done anything to us! Give him a chance!"

Sherbrooke, Quebec, August 20.—Harry K. Thaw will be across the American border in the state of Vermont by tomorrow night if tomorrow's events in this case of the fugitive from Matteawan shape themselves as Canadian officials in close touch with the proceedings anticipate.

This was the semi-official intimation here tonight as Thaw awaits a hearing on the habeas corpus writ his counsel secured today.

It is not denied that official opinion inclines to the belief that the habeas corpus proceedings will result in Thaw being declared a free man. What will follow, then, is a matter of the immigration authorities indicate, lies in the hands of Inspectors D. B. Reynolds and F. R. Whatham, of Ottawa. These two officials, immediately Thaw is released by the court, it is understood, will take him into custody as an undesirable alien—the immigration act and oust the fugitive to Canada.

At the immigration office the formal deportation proceedings will be conducted in the form of an official inquiry into the manner of Thaw's entrance into the country, and his past history, which it is held debars him from remaining in Canada.

To Drop Thaw in Vermont.

Three formalities ended, he will be taken on board a Grand Trunk train and conveyed to the border, where Messrs. Reynolds and Whatham will hand him over to the American authorities.

The point of deportation indicated will be Island Pond, Vermont, the nearest border station on the Grand Trunk, about twenty miles south of Coaticook.

The "through ticket" to Detroit, on which Thaw, it is understood, hopes to evade the immigration authorities and continue his journey through Quebec and Ontario to the state of Michigan, will not serve that purpose, if the information of the immigration officials is correct. Though they have not yet been shown the ticket by Thaw, they have learned that it was purchased in Coaticook and reads from that point to Detroit. It is not, therefore, a ticket over the American station, via Canada, to another foreign point, and does not qualify as "through" transportation.

The possible hitch is that the deportation plan would be a further with of habeas corpus calling upon the immigration authorities to show cause why Thaw is not eligible to enter Canada. This would further delay action.

Further such a situation, Stanford White's erratic slayer, ordinarily loquacious, has shut his lips tight and said the girl tempted him.

He may serve twenty years in the pen for taking Marsha Warrington from Sacramento, Cal., to Reno, Nev. Diggs told a he jury it was just an "escapade" and said the girl tempted him.

Continued on Page Fourteen

THIS IS DIGGS.

MAURY DIGGS

Girls Tell Jury Frank's Character Is Bad

Photo by Francis E. Price, Staff Photographer.

Miss Myrtice Cato and Miss Maggie Griffin.

NEGRESS GARBED AS MAN SHOOTS JOHN F. HALL

After Wounding the Turpentine Operator She Kills Herself.

Savannah, Ga., August 20.—John F. Hall, a prominent turpentine operator living near Hinesboro, Ga., was shot in the leg last night by a negro woman dressed in man's clothing. After shooting Mr. Hall the woman took poison, ending her life. The coroner's verdict was suicide.

There were six counts in the indictment, and the jury found a verdict of guilty on the first four. Each count carries a maximum penalty of five years and a minimum of one year in a federal penitentiary.

SON DISCOVERS FATHER TAKING LIFE WITH GAS

Quick Medical Attention Saves Lawrence Louis, of Hazlehurst, From Death.

Hazlehurst, Ga., August 20.—Seated in a chair with a rubber tube between his lips while one from a stove poured into his lungs, Lawrence Louis, who conducts a restaurant on West Broad street, was found in an unconscious condition early this morning when his son, Robert Louis broke into his store. The elder Louis was hurried to the Savannah hospital in the police ambulance, and, although physicians have been working on him almost incessantly, his condition is yet uncertain.

Relatives of Louis know, that his act this morning was an effort to end his life. They attribute mental worry as the cause.

Louis has two sons who are in ill health. In addition he has been worried over the condition of his business. Despondency over the condition it believed to have made him decide to end his life.

SEVENTEENTH BABY CAUSED HER DEATH

Columbus, Ohio, August 20.—Following the birth of her seventeenth child, Mrs. John O'Donnell, aged 38, of this city, died at a local hospital. Shortly before her death Mrs. O'Donnell, received word of the death of her sister, Mrs. Mary Pullen, of Washington Courthouse, Ohio.

Harry Murphy, of this city, a nephew of Mrs. O'Donnell, also died today. Mrs O'Donnell is survived by her husband and eight of their children. O'Donnell is the father of twenty-eight children, eleven having been born during a former marriage.

Weather Prophecy
FAIR

Georgia: Fair Thursday and Friday; moderate northeast winds.

Local Report.

Lowest temperature	.70
Highest temperature	.79
Mean temperature	.74
Normal temperature	.78
Deficiency for the day	.4
Deficiency since Aug. 1	.none
Deficiency since Jan. 1, inches	2.12

Reports From Various Stations.

STATIONS	Tem'p		Rain
STATE OF WEATHER	7 p.m.	Max.	
Atlanta, cloudy	.78	.79	.00
Atlantic City, p.c.	.74	.76	.00
Baltimore, clear	.74	.82	.00
Birmingham, clr	.78	.84	.00
Boise City, clear	.70	.84	.00
Boston, clear	.68	.76	.00
Brownsville, cl'r	.80	.84	.00
Buffalo, clear	.66	.72	.00
Charleston, clr	.78	.84	.00
Chicago, pt. cldy	.68	.76	.00
Denver, cloudy	.62	.72	.00
Galveston, clear	.80	.84	.00
Jacksonville, clear	.80	.86	.00
Kansas City, clr	.66	.78	.00
Knoxville, rain	.74	.80	.20
Louisville, cloudy	.72	.78	.00
Memphis, clear	.74	.82	.00
Miami, clear	.80	.84	.00
Montgomery, clr	.78	.84	.00
New Orleans, clr	.80	.84	.00
Oklahoma, clear	.72	.84	.00
Pittsburg, clear	.68	.76	.00
Portland, clear	.60	.72	.00
Raleigh, cloudy	.74	.82	.00
San Francisco, clr	.58	.64	.00
St. Louis, cloudy	.70	.78	.00
St. Paul, clear	.62	.72	.00
Salt Lake City, clr	.66	.84	.00
Seattle, cloudy	.58	.70	.00
Shreveport, pt. cldy	.80	.86	.00
Tampa, pt. cloudy	.80	.86	.00
Toledo, clear	.66	.74	.00
Washington, clear	.74	.82	.00

C. F. von HERRMANN, Section Director.

HOTEL AT UNION CITY DESTROYED BY FLAMES

25 Guests of the Reid House Narrowly Escape Cremation.

Union City, Ga., August 20.—(Special)—The twenty-five guests of the Reid hotel at this place narrowly escaped from death this morning when the fire was discovered in the building. Within a few minutes after the fire call was sounded the hotel was a mass of flames, and nothing but a few personal effects were saved.

Valiant work on the part of the volunteer fire department saved the office building of the farmers' union, a frame story 310,000 brick structure, next to the hotel. The Reid hotel was a frame structure, valued at $4,500. Fire was caused by a defective flue, it is said.

TRIAL NEARING END AND LEO M. FRANK SHOULD KNOW FATE BY NEXT SATURDAY

Shortly After 4 O'Clock Wednesday Afternoon the State Announced Closed—There Was a Short Discussion About Admission of Certain Documentary Evidence, and Prisoner Was Then Put Back on Stand to Give Him Opportunity to Deny Certain Statements Made by Witnesses After His Story Told to Jury on Tuesday Afternoon.

FRANK HOOPER OPENS FOR THE STATE TODAY; NO TIME LIMIT IS SET

State Renewed Its Pitiless Attack on Frank's Character Early in Morning, and Some Ten or More Girls Who Once Worked at National Pencil Factory Swore That Character of Superintendent Was Bad—Two Testified They Had Seen Frank Go Into Dressing Room With Girl Who Had Testified for the Defense.

The Frank trial has enter'd in its last lap leg.

Saturday should write finis to the most famous case in the annals of Georgia crime, and Leo M. Frank should know his fate.

Hundreds of witnesses have been on the stand to give testimony for and against Frank. They have withstood the fire of cross-examination of failed beneath the hacked shafts of pointed questions. Experts have disagreed and wrangled on the fundamentals of the human system; character witnesses have judged Frank as a paragon of the virtues or pictured him as a man utterly devoid of the elements of common decency. A white man of college education and hitherto spotless reputation has been pitted against an ignorant negro whose is no stranger to crime and the chaingang. A city of over 150,000 souls has been divided on the subject of the white man's or the negro's guilt or innocence.

END OF IT ALL NEAR AT HAND.

The end of it all is near. The city looks forward with relief to the verdict—whatever it may be—by the people of Atlanta have centered their attention on this trial as never before in history.

The verdict?

No man can answer the question. Time alone, which has been taking toll of the seconds and minutes and hours and days and weeks of the trial, can tell. The faces of the jurors who sit through the interminable hours of question and cross-examination of quibble and of contention are as masques which completely hide their emotion. No human being can peer within and read the mis ms of these men. Maybap they have made up their minds. Again, it may be they are waiting for the argument—the

Continued on Page Twelve.

U. S. JUDGE SPEER MAY LOSE POSITION BY IMPEACHMENT

Serious Charges, Presented by Department of Justice, Are Being Considered by House Judiciary Committee.

WASTING OF ESTATES CHARGED TO THE JUDGE

One Allegation Says Speer Named Son-in-Law Bankruptcy Referee and Awarded Exorbitant Fees.

Washington, August 20.—Charges which, if sustained, may be the foundation of another impeachment case in the senate are made against Federal Judge Emory Speer, of the fifth Georgia circuit, in papers considered today in a carefully guarded session of the house judiciary committee.

The committee had before it the report of an investigation into Judge Speer's conduct by Special Examiner R. C. Lewis, submitted by the department of justice, along with numerous affidavits and other exhibits. No action was taken, the committee adjourning until Friday, and each member pledging himself not to discuss the charges in the meantime.

It is possible that at Friday's session of the house the matter may be formally brought up with a view of outlining a plan of action by the committee in the event it should determine to report the charges to the house, either favorably or unfavorably.

Two Serious Charges Against Speer.

The most serious charges dealt with in the examiner's report are:

That Judge Speer unlawfully permitted the wasting or dissipation of bankruptcy estates that came within his jurisdiction as a federal judge.

That he presided in cases in which his son-in-law was an attorney or a contingent fee, with full knowledge that his decision would affect the fee of his son-in-law.

That he was guilty of imposing unlawful punishments for contempt in cases coming before his court.

That he ignored the mandates of the circuit court of appeals.

Continued on Page Twelve.

As the prosecution closed its case, the newspapers kept up a steady supply of words and images about the trial. This front page from the August 21 *Constitution* featured photos of the teenage witnesses against Frank, making them local celebrities for a time.

"STATE ADDS LINKS TO CHAIN." The defense called for a mistrial on the grounds that the headline could bias the jury and lead to an unfair verdict. Instead, the judge instructed the jury to disregard the headline. Even though the defense didn't feel this was adequate, they finally accepted the ruling since they expected to win the case.

While the court was recessed for Sunday, Jim Conley's attorney, William Smith, prepared his client to testify the next day. He arranged for a shave and a haircut for Conley, and police officers cleaned the man up. Conley came into court on Monday morning in a new suit, looking tidy and respectable. He fleshed out his earlier (third) affidavit on the stand, introducing a code of stomps by which he was supposed to warn his boss that someone was coming. He also described previous encounters between Leo Frank and other girls on other Saturdays, including details of witnessing oral sex—an act which was considered a particularly degrading perversion at that time.

When he got to April 26, Conley stated that Frank had told him, "I wanted to be with the little girl, and she refused me, and I struck her and I guess I struck her too hard and she fell and hit her head against something, and I don't know how bad she got hurt. Of course, you know I ain't built like other men."

Although both Dorsey and his witnesses took care never to be more specific, 1913 listeners understood the unspoken implications of engaging in oral sex and not being "built like other men." The prosecution was insinuating that because Leo was Jewish, his genitals were deformed to the point that he could not enjoy conventional vaginal intercourse and could only experience sexual pleasure in ways that were then considered perverted.

This false, prejudiced idea had been widely held by anti-Semites for centuries, perhaps fueled by misunderstandings about the Jewish tradition of circumcision. But no one put the accusation into plain words at the trial, so it was impossible for Leo's lawyers to refute as a complete fabrication born out of ignorance and bigotry.

Having planted the seeds of Leo's perversion leading to a deliberate sexual attack on Mary, Conley went on to describe the cover-up. He said he had carried Mary's body onto the elevator and down to the basement with Leo's help and then wrote the letters that Leo dictated.

THE ATLANTA CONSTITUTION
THE STANDARD SOUTHERN NEWSPAPER.

Vol. XLVI.—No. 50.　　　ATLANTA, GA. TUESDAY MORNING, AUGUST 5, 1913.—EIGHTEEN PAGES.　　　Daily and Sunday, carrier delivery, 12 cents weekly. Single copies on the streets and at newsstands, 5 cents.

CONLEY GRILLED FIVE HOURS BY LUTHER ROSSER

PRESSURE BROUGHT BY UNITED STATES TO DEPOSE HUERTA

Ambassador Wilson Resigns and Ex-Gov. Lind Is Ordered to Mexico as Personal Agent of President.

MEXICANS TO BE TOLD HUERTA MUST ABDICATE

Believed American Ban on Huerta May Force Resignation—Henry L. Wilson Asked to Keep Out of Mexico.

Washington, August 4.—President Wilson today took the first steps in the policy through which he proposes to deal with the Mexican situation. He formally accepted the resignation of Ambassador Henry Lane Wilson, to take effect on October 14, and sent to Mexico City as his personal representative—but not accredited to the Huerta government—former Governor John Lind, of Minnesota, a lifelong friend of Secretary Bryan. The understanding is that when a stable government is established Mr. Lane Wilson will be formally named as ambassador.

Lind's Mission Announced.

President Wilson and Secretary Bryan had frequent conferences during the day; afterwards Wilson had a long talk with Mr. Bryan and Chairman Bacon, of the senate foreign relations committee, discussed the situation with the president at the white house. But for the announcement of Mr. Lind's mission, no explanation of the policy to be pursued by the American government was forthcoming. The statement from Secretary Bryan of Mr. Lind's mission, has been sent to numerous governments.

Meanwhile news and munitions of war from the United States will continue to be denied to the two warring forces and unless it is apparent that internal efforts to bring about peace have failed the United States will not offer its services as a mediator. Mr. Lind undoubtedly will act in that capacity when the time comes.

Declarations from both Huerta and

Continued on Last Page.

There's Only One Way To Do a Thing.

That's the right way. And the right way is usually the easiest and surest way.

When you want clothes you go to a shop that sells them and buy what you want.

When you want a job you should follow similar tactics. Go where the jobs are offered. Read The Constitution want ads every day—

And use Constitution want ads every day—until you find the job you want.

There's no keeping you down if you're sincere. Others have found the right place through The Constitution want. There's no reason why you cannot do likewise.

Your ad in this paper carries weight with the business men of Atlanta because they know you pay for it. All of which only means that being a business man you're in business way.

"You Can't Get Something for Nothing."

SENATE INDORSES CUT OF $280,325 IN MONEY SHEET

Upholds Action of Committee in Making Outgo of State Equal to Income by Chopping 7 Per Cent Off Figures.

SENATORS VOTE TODAY ON PENSION DECREASE

All Other Amendments Are Agreed To on Monday. University Accepts Smaller Appropriation.

The state senate completed half of the general appropriations bill as amended by the appropriation committee yesterday afternoon. There were many amendments offered to the bill and to the committee's amendments, but in every instance the action of the committee was sustained by a business majority.

The most animated fights of the day came over the amendment of Senator E. L. Smith, of the sixth, to completely strike the section giving $30,000 to the State Medical college at Augusta and the effort of Senator M. C. Tarver, of the forty-third, to cut the appropriation to the Georgia Tech from $90,000 to $20,000 instead of $74,400 as recommended by the committee. Both of these attempts were lost.

Committee Amendments Adopted.

The following amendments of the committee were passed:

University of Georgia, $53,000 to $48,722.

Georgia Tech, $90,000 to $74,400.

Georgia Normal and Industrial college, $52,500 to $48,722.

Agricultural college at Dahlonega, $21,588 to $19,895.

State Normal school at Athens $47,500 to $44,172.

State College of Agriculture, $200,000 to $52,000.

Medical College, $30,000 to $17,500.

Common school fund, $2,558,000 to $1,517,500.

Pensions due to increase of population School fund and Dumb, $450.

The following other amendments were passed:

By Senator Tarver, of the forty-third, to increase the number of directors in the house of representatives from three to four.

Amendments Lost 21 to 12.

The amendment of Senator Olliff, of the fourth, to the committee's amendment, providing that the cut in the common school fund shall only be from $2,558,000 to $1,500,000, was lost by a vote of 21 to 12 after a lively debate. Senator Olliff deplored the fact that the poor people of the state were made to suffer at the hands of the state, while certain schools of higher education were given the same amount as they have been getting or even more in view of the fact that 1 per cent was cut from their appropriation which was raised in the house.

In all this the amount was 7 per cent of that given by the house and those institutions which had been granted a larger sum by the house amended themselves only the commission remains to be considered, the cut from $350,000 to $210,000 in the pension fund, and judging from the sources in which the senate supported its committee Monday this decrease will in all probability be made today.

Only One Amendment Probable.

Although many amendments have been sent to the desk, it is probable that the amendment of the committee decreasing the pension fund will be the only one that is passed by the senate today. If the bill is passed as amended by the committee and five from other amendments, it will cut from the present appropriations bill the sum of $290,325, approximately the same amount which is in excess of the anticipated revenue.

Probably the most striking incident of the session occurred when Senator E. T. DuBose, of the thirtieth district and a resident of Athens, made a short talk to the upper house covering the motion to cut the maintenance fund of the University of Georgia from $53,000 to $48,722.

Senator DuBose stated that he knew that the University of Georgia was perfectly willing to give up that share of money along with the other state institutions in the interest of the betterment of the financial condition of the state. "Of course," said he, "the university needs the money as much, if not more than most of our educational institutions, but at the same time when a serious crisis is facing our state I know it is willing to sacrifice itself for the state."

The amendment striking the $30,000 from the Augusta Medical college was lost by a vote of 28 to 4.

Senator Smith, of the sixth district, in support of his amendment striking the appropriation of $30,000 to the Augusta Medical college, among other things, said: "At the last session of the legislature the trustees of this college came before the legislature and offered this college to the state as a gift, and, I understand, that they stated they would ask for an appropriation. The commissions recognized the fact that trading centers and trade routes existed long before the establishment of railroads. This was recognized in fixing rates to be continued.

Continued on Page Five.

Scenes in Courtroom Monday While Conley Was on Stand

"JIM, CAN YOU PUT THIS COP AROUND YOUR NECK LIKE YOU FOUND IT ON MARY'S BODY?"

WOMEN SPECTATORS

JIM CONLEY
On the STAND.

RATE CASES WON BY GEORGIA TOWNS

Freight Rates to LaGrange, Carrollton and Vienna Declared Unjust—Will Cost Railroads $4,000,000 Year.

Washington, August 4.—(Special.)—Commissioner Clements, in rendering the decision of the interstate commerce commission today in the LaGrange, Carrollton and Vienna, rate cases, condemned the existing arbitrary differences in rates to these points as compared with rates to Atlanta and Cedartown, the basing points.

The decision of the commission is of tremendous importance. It will cause a readjustment of rates throughout the south, and it is estimated to mean a loss to the railroads of $4,000,000 or $5,000,000 a year, or a reduction of 10 per cent.

The decision does not prohibit lower rates to basing points which have water competition, but in declining such, by reason of competition has been perpetrated, it does condemn the existing so-called "arbitraries," or differences above the rates to basing points, and "differentials," or differences below the basing rates.

How Southern Rates Are Based.

All rates to the south from the east are based on the rates from Baltimore and Louisville to Atlanta. The commission finds that the arbitrary increase of 77 cents to Carrollton, as compared with the Louisville-Atlanta rate to too high by 13 cents. It holds the arbitrary increase of 26 cents over the Baltimore-Atlanta rate to LaGrange by 5 cents.

In other words, taking the rail and water rates from Baltimore and Louisville, as controlling all these routes to decides that the differentials shall not exceed 12 cents from east to west and that the arbitraries shall not exceed 12 cents. The basing point system of making rates is not condemned but the commissions recognized the fact that trading centers and trade routes existed long before the establishment of railroads. This was recognized in fixing rates to be continued.

Continued on Page Five.

How Atlanta Is Affected By the New Express Rates

By John Corrigan, Jr.

Washington, August 4.—(Special.)—Atlanta is a selected list of cities, ordered by the interstate commerce commission, to become effective October 15. The rates ordered by the commission will undoubtedly be used as an argument for further reducing the parcel post rates. It is predicted that within five years the express companies will have been abolished entirely.

The figures given below are a comparison of the present parcel post rates, present express rates and new express rates for packages weighing one, five and ten pounds. The last two columns are the present express rates and new express rates on 100 pounds of merchandise.

The new limit for parcel post packages is twenty pounds, but this increase was ordered after the interstate commerce commission had made up its table of comparisons and these are not carried beyond the former eleven-pound parcel post limit.

From Atlanta to	1 Pound		5 Pounds			10 Pounds			100 Pounds	
	PARCEL POST	NEW	PARCEL POST	OLD	NEW	PARCEL POST	OLD	NEW	OLD	NEW
Jacksonville	.07	.25	.27	.35	.47	.42	1.60	.35	2.35	1.75
Chicago	.09	.28	.29	.55	.52	.57	1.88	.70	3.00	2.10
St. Louis	.09	.25	.29	.52	.51	.57	2.75	.65	3.45	2.45
Nashville	.07	.25	.27	.35	.47	.42	1.40	.55	1.60	1.65
New Orleans	.08	.25	.28	.45	.49	.51	.80	.65	2.55	1.95
Augusta, Maine	.09	.30	.30	.75	.57	.75	1.30	.95	3.75	2.85
Denver	.10	.30	.32	.75	.60	.80	3.50	.95	4.75	3.55
Spokane	.12	.30	.34	.75	.66	.80	4.00	.95	6.00	4.60
Duluth	.10	.25	.32	.75	.55	.80	3.00	.65	4.00	2.90

NEGRO IS SOUGHT BY ARMED WHITES

Residents of Lampkin Street and Vicinity Stirred by Attempted Assault Upon Girl 11 Years Old.

As the result of an attempted assault upon a little white girl 11 years of age, Lenn Green, a negro, was sought for hours last night by a large crowd of white men.

The attack took place in the home of the negro at 19 Lampkin street. Mrs. Green, wife of the negro, was out in her back yard when she heard the scream of a little girl, who lived in the vicinity of the negro's home, and when she opened the door to see what was the matter she saw the negro and the white girl struggling in the yard. She immediately began to struggle, and made no outcry. Although of small stature, the girl succeeded in frustrating the negro's evil designs for perhaps ten minutes, when he became frightened and released her.

The little girl sped swiftly up the street to the home of her sister, where she sobbingly poured out the pitiful story. Police were notified and officers were hastily dispatched to the scene, but the negro could not be found.

In the meantime, a determined body of men, heavily armed with a rope and headed by the near neighbors of the little girl, were piling out into the street for blocks in the vicinity of the home of the negro, and he was every indication that had he been captured Green would doubtless have met death

Continued on Page Five.

SENATE WAITING FOR HOUSE BILL

Will Start Work on Revision When Sheppard Substitute Is Transmitted — No Reconsideration.

There was no reconsideration of the Sheppard substitute by the house yesterday and the bill should be ingrossed in the house to be transmitted to the senate today.

Chairman Miller, of the senate finance committee said that his committee was waiting for the bill and would go to work on it just as soon as it is received from the house. It all depends upon the time required to copy the bill by one of the engrossing clerks of the house, and there seems to be no reason why the measure may not reach the senate today.

In speaking on the subject of tax reform, Senator Miller said:

"It has not yet been determined whether or not the house will vote on an empty amended or passed by extra statute in the senate. It will set up through the finance committees without some provision being made for a tax commission or some form of state board to supervise the returns of the whole state. I do not believe that the senate will accept a bill that makes no better provision for reconsideration than merely county boards of equalizers."

Motion to Reconsider Withdrawn.

When the house met yesterday morning Representative McMichael, of Marion, who had given notice of a motion to reconsider the Sheppard measure, asked the unanimous consent of the house to withdraw his motion so that the bill might be transmitted to the senate earlier. This was granted and there was no further effort made to reconsider the bill.

An effort will be made to have the senate finance committee adopt the substance of the Sheppard bill as

Continued on Page Five.

REMARKABLE STORY IS TOLD BY NEGRO IN ACCUSING FRANK OF PHAGAN MURDER

Chief Witness for State Admits, Under Cross-Examination, That He Has Been Under Arrest Seven or Eight Times, and That Many Statements Made in His Three Affidavits Are False. Hangs His Head and "Fools With His Fingers" When He Lies, He Says.

LOOPS MURDER NOOSE AROUND HIS OWN NECK TO ILLUSTRATE STORY

By Order of Judge the Court Is Cleared of Women and Children at Afternoon Session Owing to Revolting Testimony Given by Conley—Dr. Roy Harris, It Is Understood, Will Be Closing Witness Summoned by the Prosecution.

The long-looked-for sensation in the Leo M. Frank trial came Monday morning when Jim Conley, the negro sweeper formerly employed at the National Pencil factory, took the stand and told a revolting, as well as dramatic story of what he claims to know of the murder of little Mary Phagan.

Following the telling of this story, parts of which can only be hinted at, Conley was placed under cross-examination by Luther Rosser. For five hours and a half the able attorney for the defense wheedled and coaxed and cajoled and used every tactic known to the legal profession to break down the fabric of the story and to tear the tale to tatters.

He succeeded in confusing the negro as to minor details only. He failed to shake the foundation of the main story—which was that on Saturday, April 25, Leo M. Frank had asked him to "look out" for him while he "chatted" with a young woman; that later Frank had called to him and told him the girl had "refused him" and that he had struck her. He then described seeing the body of the girl lying on the floor near her machine with a cord and a piece of cloth around her neck. She was dead.

Asked Him to Help.

He recited that Frank had asked him to help him dispose of the body and that he had taken it to the basement. He told of Frank's plan to have him burn the body. He told of writing the notes which were later found near the body.

These things he told in a fashion so rapid it was difficult for the stenographers to follow him. During the

Weather Prophecy
GENERALLY FAIR

Georgia—Fair Tuesday and probably Wednesday; light to moderate variable winds.

Local Report.

Rosser cross-examined Conley Monday afternoon and all day Tuesday but could not shake him in his story beyond getting him to admit he had lied to the police in the beginning. Conley seemed to enjoy answering the attorney's questions. At one point, Rosser challenged the size of a piece of cloth that Conley claimed to have used in moving Mary's body:

"Well, what do you call two feet?"

"This is what I call two feet," cried Conley, putting the toe of his right shoe against the heel of his left and lifting them high off the floor.

Jim Conley's flippant answers did not weaken his credibility for the all-white jury. Nor did his admission that he had initially lied to the police. In 1913 most juries, particularly in the South, assumed that a black man was less likely to tell the truth than a white man. Having him admit that he had lied but was now telling the truth actually made him more believable, as did his cockiness.

Realizing that Conley had seriously damaged Leo's case, the defense made a motion to exclude parts of his testimony. They wanted the judge to instruct the jury to disregard what Conley had said about watching for anyone who might interrupt Leo when he was with a girl and also his testimony that Leo was not "built like other men." Dorsey insisted that the evidence went to the heart of who had killed Mary and why. He pointed out that if the defense had wanted to object, they should have done it immediately, not after they had cross-examined Conley unsuccessfully for over eight hours.

After a spirited argument, during which the jury was out of the room, Judge Roan ruled that Jim Conley's testimony was admissible. The people in the courtroom applauded loudly, and the mob in the streets erupted in cheers. Arnold again asked for a mistrial, stating that crowd reaction prejudiced their case. Judge Roan denied the motion on the grounds that the jury was not present and therefore had not heard it. But of course, the jury could hear the cheers and applause. Anyone in the building could hear the mob through the open windows.

The prosecution's last witness was C. Brutus Dalton, a carpenter who testified that Jim Conley had kept watch for both Leo and

Dalton himself while they met with women in Leo's office and in the factory basement. On cross-examination, Rosser tripped up Dalton in several lies and got him to admit that he was a convict. Nevertheless, when the prosecution rested, the *Georgian* reported, "One by one the prosecutor has forged the links in the chain that he maintains fixes the guilt of the Phagan murder on Leo Frank and Leo Frank alone." Leo's defense team faced a much harder task in the second half of the trial than they'd anticipated.

"THERE CAN BE BUT ONE VERDICT"

THE DEFENSE RESTS

While the job of the prosecution was to present evidence to convict the accused, the job of the defense was to disprove that evidence or at least convince the jury that there was reasonable doubt that their client could be guilty. Leo's defense started strong, presenting Dr. Leroy Childs, who described how hard cabbage was to digest. Dr. Childs testified that Mary had probably been killed more than thirty or forty-five minutes after she ate, refuting Dr. Harris's claim. This medical testimony rendered the prosecution's entire timeline invalid.

Next, the defense recalled Pinkerton detective Harry Scott and used his reluctant testimony to show the jury how Scott and the police had coached Jim Conley. While this was a technical victory, it had none of the emotional impact of Conley's original testimony about Leo's alleged sexual encounters and perversions.

Rosser and Arnold continued to present reasoned testimony that refuted each detail of the prosecution's evidence. One of the girls that Dalton had accused of going up to Leo's office with him testified that she had never done so. The motorman who had driven the streetcar that took Mary to the factory on the day of her death testified that no one had sat beside her or talked to her. This refuted George Epps's testimony that he had ridden with Mary and his earlier statements that she'd told him she was afraid of Leo Frank. And the conductor testified that Mary had gotten off the streetcar at 12:10. This contradicted Jim Conley's testimony about when the girl had arrived and made Monteen Stover's testimony about Leo not being in his office when she was there looking for him between 12:05 and 12:10 irrelevant. The prosecution's timeline was crumbling.

But the defense's performance in drawing such significant information out of their witnesses was too cool and collected to convince the jury. The only impassioned moments were when Hugh Dorsey leaped to his feet to cross-examine witnesses, scoring only minor points but making them sound hugely impressive. The defense had not been able to track down Will Green, who could testify that Conley had been the real killer, and for reasons they never explained, they chose not to put William Mincey on the stand to testify that Conley had told him he had killed a girl on Confederate Memorial Day. Without eyewitnesses of their own to disprove Conley's eyewitness testimony, the defense failed to make a strong impact on either the crowd or the jury.

Other witnesses testified about the layout of the rooms and floors in the factory, about the door that had been found broken in the basement after the murder, and about the habits of other employees in coming in and out of the factory on Saturdays. Assistant Superintendent Herbert Schiff testified that Harry Scott, the Pinkerton agent hired by the National Pencil Company, had stated explicitly that the agency wanted Frank found guilty and had been working in collusion with the police the whole time.

Schiff also gave detailed testimony about Jim Conley's tendency to lie, saying that the company kept him on only because it was hard to find janitors who would show up for work reliably. Then Schiff compared the amount and quality of the paperwork Leo had completed on April 26 with the reports he had prepared on previous Saturdays and said that the work was identical. He said this indicated that Leo had been in a normal frame of mind and working as usual that day—making it seem unlikely that he killed someone in the

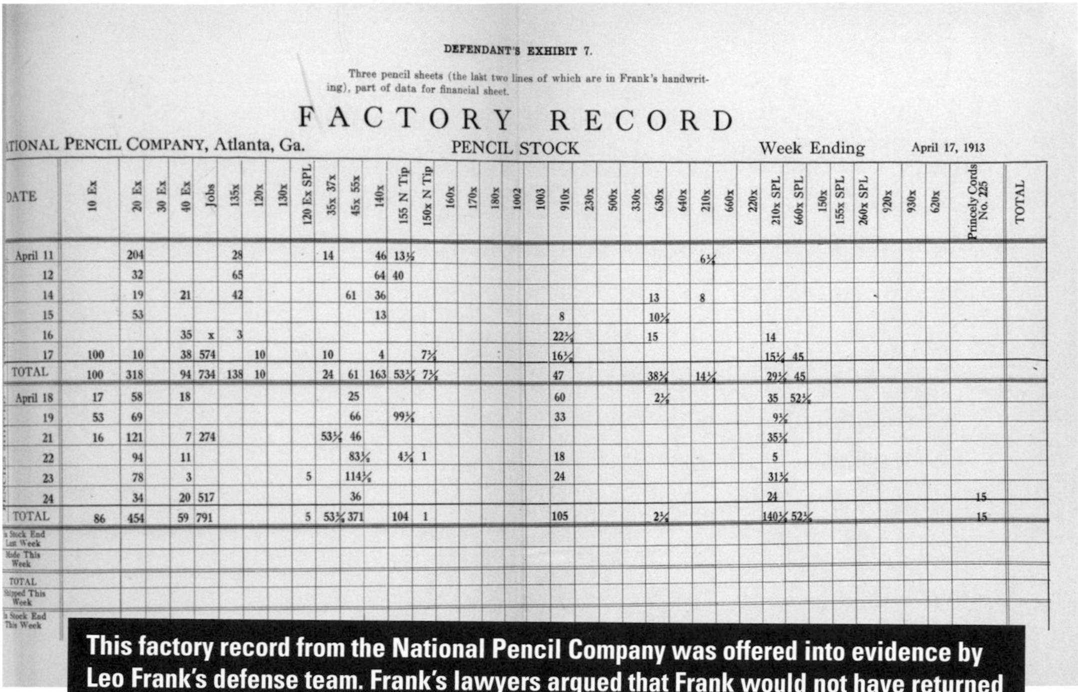

DEFENDANT'S EXHIBIT 7.

Three pencil sheets (the last two lines of which are in Frank's handwriting), part of data for financial sheet.

FACTORY RECORD

[NA]TIONAL PENCIL COMPANY, Atlanta, Ga. PENCIL STOCK Week Ending April 17, 1913

DATE	10 Ex	20 Ex	30 Ex	40 Ex	Jobs	135x	120x	130x	120 Ex SPL	35x 37x	45x 55x	140x	155 N Tip	150x N Tip	160x	170x	180x	1002	1003
April 11		204				28				14		46	13½						
12		32				65						64	40						
14		19		21		42					61	36							
15		53										13							
16				35	x	3													
17	100	10		38	574		10			10		4		7½					
TOTAL	100	318		94	734	138	10			24	61	163	53½	7½					
April 18	17	58		18							25								
19	53	69									66		99¾						
21	16	121		7	274					53¼	46								
22		94		11							83⅛		4¾	1					
23		78		3					5		114⅛								
24		34		20	517						36								
TOTAL	86	454		59	791				5	53¼	371		104	1					
[In] Stock End Last Week																			
Made This Week																			
TOTAL Shipped This Week																			
[In] Stock End This Week																			

DATE	910x	230x	500x	330x	630x	640x	210x	660x	220x	210x SPL	660x SPL	150x	155x SPL	260x SPL	920x	930x	620x	Princely Cords No. 225	TOTAL
April 11							6¼												
12																			
14					13		8												
15	8				10¾														
16	22½				15					14									
17	16½									15¼	45								
TOTAL	47				38¾		14¼			29¾	45								
April 18	60				2½					35	52½								
19	33									9½									
21										35½									
22	18									5									
23	24									31½									
24										24								15	
TOTAL	105				2½					140½	52½							15	
[In] Stock End Last Week																			
Made This Week																			
TOTAL Shipped This Week																			
[In] Stock End This Week																			

This factory record from the National Pencil Company was offered into evidence by Leo Frank's defense team. Frank's lawyers argued that Frank would not have returned to complicated paperwork if he had just raped and murdered Mary Phagan.

midst of his weekend bookkeeping and was then able to remain calm and routine at the job.

Fourteen-year-old Magnolia Kennedy refuted Helen Ferguson's claim that Leo had refused to give her Mary's pay so he could see the girl on Saturday. Magnolia confirmed that Mary had not been present on payday, and testified that she (Magnolia) was right behind Helen when the conversation allegedly took place. Not only did Helen not ask for Mary's money at all, but it was Herbert Schiff who paid the workers that day, not Leo Frank, so there was no possible way that Leo could have attempted to arrange a meeting with Mary on Saturday.

Two of the office boys who had worked at the factory also testified for the defense: fourteen-year-old Alonzo Mann and fifteen-year-old Philip Chambers. Alonzo shyly testified in a low voice that he had never seen C. Brutus Dalton going up to the superintendent's office with women or any women going into the superintendent's office at all, but he appeared nervous. A reporter wrote, "He was frightened by his experience in court, and the stenographer [court reporter] had difficulty in hearing his answers."

Philip Chambers, on the other hand, was a confident witness, firmly insisting that he had never seen the superintendent acting familiar with any of the women in the factory. Dorsey only cross-examined Alonzo briefly, not wanting to make the court feel sympathetic toward the already anxious witness, but he went after Philip with vigor. Dorsey not only challenged the boy about Leo's alleged relationships with female employees but implied that the superintendent had made improper advances to Philip himself. The implication that Leo was a pedophile who had tried to have homosexual relations with his young male employees, as well as depraved sexual relations with his young female employees, was even more horrifying to 1913 society than it would be today.

Philip flatly denied the suggestion, and Arnold objected furiously, announcing, "If courts were run this way it could be brought against any member of the community—you, me, or the jury. No man can get a fair showing against such vile insinuations. If this comes up again, I will be tempted to move for a new trial."

Judge Roan had the cross-examination erased from the record, but the jurors had heard it, just as they had heard the crowd's response to the decision not to exclude Jim Conley's testimony. Jurors are required to disregard any information that the judge orders them not to consider, but the defense feared that would be impossible in such an emotionally charged atmosphere.

Throughout the third week of the trial, the defense continued to call witnesses who systematically disproved the prosecution's case. Dorsey refrained from cross-examining some of the women witnesses, but not all. He attacked Minola McKnight after she testified about being forced by police to sign the false affidavit. He also criticized Leo's mother-in-law, arguing that Mrs. Selig should have been more concerned about Mary's murder in her son-in-law's factory the Sunday the body was found. Dorsey shrugged off the fact that Mrs. Selig had been ill and had gone in for an operation the following day. He wanted the jury to believe that this Jewish high-society family couldn't care less about the death of some working girl they didn't know.

The defense would call several more witnesses from the factory to support their contention that Jim Conley had taken Mary into the

THE STANDARD SOUTHERN NEWSPAPER

THE ATLANTA CONSTITUTION

THE STANDARD SOUTHERN NEWSPAPER

Vol. XLVI—No. 53.　　　ATLANTA, GA. FRIDAY MORNING, AUGUST 8, 1913.—SIXTEEN PAGES.　　　Daily and Sunday, carrier delivery, 12 cents weekly.
Single copies on the streets and at all newsstands, 5 cents.

DEFENSE MAY CALL FOR CHARACTER WITNESSES TODAY

MEXIC SITUATION GRAVE; GEN. HUERTA'S DEFIANCE MAY RESULT IN TROUBLE

Official Washington Regards Situation as Even Graver Than That Which Preceded the War With Spain.

PRESIDENT REALIZES GRAVITY OF THE CASE, BUT HOPES FOR PEACE

Wilson Regards as Almost Incredible Some of the Statements Issued on Behalf of Huerta—Huerta's Course May Drive United States to Recognize His Foes.

Washington, August 7.—The American government tonight was confronted by what official Washington regarded as the most delicate situation in its relations with Mexico that has yet developed since armed revolution disturbed the peace of the southern republic.

The threatened rebuff from the Huerta administration to the mission of John Lind, personal representative of President Wilson, en route to Mexico City to expound the hopes of the United States for a suspension of hostilities and an orderly constitutional election in Mexico, drew from Senator Bacon, chairman of the foreign relations committee, a declaration on the floor of the senate today that the present situation was the "gravest in years, much graver than confronted us when the Cuban question was here."

WILSON REALIZES GRAVITY.

President Wilson realizes the gravity of the situation and manifested during the day his displeasure at the attitude of some members of the minority party in congress, telling callers that he believed certain indications were making it difficult for him to handle the situation in a peaceful manner.

On this account, Mr. Wilson tonight felt tonight the strong and emphatic language of Senator Bacon, who, during a debate in the senate on the resolution of Senator Fall, of Wyoming, republican, demanding a general investigation of Mexican affairs, had referred to the resolution as openly "disrespectful" and "flouting in the face of the president," while the latter was endeavoring to put into effect a peace policy. The resolution finally passed off the day's calendar.

Peaceful Solution Hoped For.

President Wilson was removed by a demur from Mexico City replacing the Huerta government as inimical to Mr. Lind's mission. He let it be known that so far as he was able to learn, there was not the slightest demand from the American people for interposition, and declined to discuss alternatives that might be put at event that the efforts of the American government to help restore peace in Mexico were rejected.

The president is confidently hopeful that a peaceful solution of the Mexican trouble can be affected. He made it plain to callers that until ability officially to the contrary would continue to regard as incredible the statements issued on behalf of President Huerta, declaring Mr. Lind's presence in Mexico undesirable. While there is little disposition to doubt the veracity of the news dispatches describing the attitude of the Huerta government against Lind there is hope among other administration officials that upon mature reflection as such intimations formally will be conveyed to the Washington administration.

Huerta Will Make Mistake.

The president is known to hold the opinion that the Huerta administration would make a vital mistake in refusing at this stage of the situation to receive an envoy from the chief executive of the United States, even though the emissary lacked diplomatic status. Mr. Lind, it was pointed out, was purposely sent without credentials as he might deal freely with propositions of all factions in Mexico, who might inquire as to the views of the Washington administration.

It is essential an abandonment of Continued on Page Seven.

You Have the Advantage of Your Father

When he was your age and wanted a job he had to go out and tramp around looking for it.

Unless some friend of his or his father knew of an opening.

But all you need to do to find a job is to read the Want Ads in The Constitution.

They are the representatives of business men who need your services and will pay you well.

Or, if you've a definite idea of what you want and don't find it advertised, go after it with a Wanted Situation Ad.

As your paid representative, it will be read by business men who know as well as you that—

"You Can't Get Something For Nothing."

THE ATLANTA CONSTITUTION

CAREY'S CONDUCT AS PARK MANAGER MAY BRING PROBE

Board Adopts Resolutions Attacking Management of Department, and Charges Before Council Are Rumored.

POLITICS BEHIND ATTACK INTIMATES PARK HEAD

Carey Says He Realizes This Is His Last Term Under Existing Conditions—Attacks Actions of Cochran.

The contracts for the electrical wiring in Piedmont park, amounting to approximately $656, have been repudiated by the park commission and Park Manager Dan Carey is charged today with charges of insubordination which are said to be brewing in council.

Following a "split" between Park President J. O. Cochran and General Manager Carey, resolutions attacking the management of the park department were offered and adopted, it voting against J. at the meeting Thursday afternoon.

Acts On Carey's Orders.

The resolution severely reprimands Manager Carey for alleged insubordinate conduct.

City Electrician R. C. Turner called for the bids in July. He asserts that he acted under instructions from Manager Carey's department.

One contract for the conduits, which lays and fixtures for the bath house, amounting to $166.25 was given to the Woodward Electric company. The Russell Electric company got a contract to put in a part of the underground system for $263.81, and the National India Rubber company was given the contract to furnish certain material, amounting to $403.10.

At his meeting President Cochran charged Manager Carey with having signed and authorized the execution of the contracts without getting the consent of the board. He makes the further charge that Manager Carey approved the vouchers and bills for the work without informing the board and that he knew at the time that there were no funds to the credit of Piedmont park with which to pay for the work. He also made the charge that Manager Carey, in entering into the contracts, violated the law and jeopardized the good name and credit of the city.

Commissioner Reynolds and Van Hosten and Councilmen Sam Shepard tend to the actions of Manager Carey.

Politics Says Carey.

"It looks to me like politics behind attack," Manager Carey says. "The board planned the work I contracted for months ago, three years, and had it not been for a misunderstanding between myself and City Electrician Turner the contracts would not have been made. President Cochran and several members of the board know that the work was being done under the contracts, but they made no effort to stop it, although it was their duty.

Manager Carey denied statements in the resolution that there are no funds in the credit of Piedmont park to pay for the work. He showed that in addition to $629 which can be used to finance the conduits and $521 which may be paid to the Southern Bell telephone company, there is a balance of $129 to the credit of the improvement fund.

Carey years ago the park board agreed to wire the bathhouse at Piedmont lake, and under resolution, Manager Carey instructed the work to be done. He secured the contract with the city electrician to bid bids. He says he merely asked Turner to call for bids, the other resolution claims that he was ordered to do the work. The resolution, however, gives the lie to that statement, and he was also instructed to have John did not read much later this afternoon. John did not read this statement as showing that it was his understanding that the work would be done and bids called for.

Manager Carey does not attempt to disguise this latest in bounds in close of City Electrician Turner. He insists that the whole affair is a misunderstanding and that he will end soon responsibility.

There is no record in the city electrician's office to show that Manager Carey ordered the work started. Turner declares that it was his understanding that the park department be ordered.

Discussing the attitude of the board, Manager Carey said:

"By adopting the resolution, the board takes the position that it does not believe my statement that the work was done through error. I have arranged through the courts to prove the fact that the underground conduit has been started in Piedmont park, but refuting that the board was guilty of negligence.

Bloody Fighting in Teheran.

Teheran, August 7.—Two more or more men were killed or wounded in street fighting between Persian troops and Bakhtiari tribesmen today. Three

Battleship Carries Special Envoy Lind to Mexico

Ex-Gov. JOHN LIND

BATTLESHIP NEW HAMPSHIRE

Ex-Governor John Lind, of Minnesota, the president's personal representative and mediator in the city of Mexico, has embarked on the United States battleship New Hampshire at Galveston for Mexico. It is estimated what the battleship would land Mr. Lind at Vera Cruz about Aug. 10, and thence he may railroad is open between Vera Cruz and the City of Mexico, and the journey usually takes about twelve hours. Mr. Lind therefore may be expected to be ready to begin his important duties the week beginning August 11. Mr. Lind will endeavor to persuade President Huerta to retire from office in advance of the holding of an election that will result in the choice of a president by constitutional means. Ex-Governor Lind has had no experience in diplomacy and has not resided in a Latin-American country. He served in the house of representatives when Wilson J. Bryan was a congressman, and his choice for the important office of mediator is credited to Mr. Bryan. During the time that he and Mr. Bryan were in congress Mr. Lind was a republican. He bolted the republican party in 1896 on account of his allegiance to free silver and came over to the democratic party in the Bryan wolf-Tarbox campaign of 1904 and the state served as a member of congress from 1903 to 1905. His home is in Minneapolis. Mr. Lind lost his left arm in an accident when he was a boy.

years ago and came to the United States when he was fourteen years old. He began the practice of law in New Ulm in 1877. He was receiver of the United States land office at Tracy, Minn., from 1881 to 1883, and member of congress from 1887 to 1893. He was elected governor of Minnesota twice.

C. B. DALTON TELLS ABOUT VISITS HE PAID THE PENCIL FACTORY WITH MANY WOMEN

Declares He Used Basement for Immoral Purposes at Same Time That Frank Was in Building, But Did Not Attempt to Say What the Superintendent's Relations With Women Were—Declares Conley Acted as Lookout for Him.

DR. LEROY W. CHILDS CALLED BY DEFENSE TO REFUTE DR. HARRIS

Harry Scott Is Also Put on Stand by Defense to Prove That Conley Lied on Many Occasions—Detective Was on the Stand When Court Adjourned for Day—Cross-Examination Fails to Shake Dr. Harris.

Shortly after Dr. H. F. Harris had completed his testimony for the state and was cross-examined its brief by Reuben Arnold, the state rested its case against Leo M. Frank.

Solicitor Dorsey had called for Frank's basis bids to show that he had in his possession approximately $200—the sum Jim Conley says he gave him and then took back—but the book was not produced, and the state rested. Later the solicitor may introduce other witnesses, but not until after the defense has closed.

Interest just now centers on the possibility of the defense introducing character witnesses, in which event the state is prepared to call several witnesses in rebuttal who otherwise could not be heard. When the trial was first called, the defense had read a long list of witnesses to prove Frank's general good character; if these witnesses are called, the trial will be drawn out for at least two weeks.

Dalton Tells Of Visits.

C. B. Dalton was the first witness called by the state Thursday morning. Dalton made a remarkably frank witness. He told of several visits he had made to the pencil factory with a Miss Daisy Hopkins and other women, and of his using the basement of the factory for immoral purposes during the time Frank was in the building with women. He did not attempt to say what the relations of Frank were with these women. He said Conley

Time for State to Pay Up, Declares Governor Slaton; Has Faith in Legislature

BOLT KILLS SON OF H. M. STANLEY

Labor Commissioner's Thirteen-Year-Old Boy, John, Found Lying Dead in Field at Dublin.

Dublin, Ga., August 1.—(Special.)—Young John Stanley, son of H. M. Stanley, commissioner of commerce and labor, was killed by lightning here this afternoon during a rain that fell about 4 o'clock. He was found dead on his face in the edge of a cotton patch near the residence of William Pritchett, whose family he had been visiting for some time.

With his brother, Harry Stanley, he was returning from a rabbit hunting to get out of the rain that was coming up. Harry reached the house of Mr. Pritchett several minutes ahead and the rain came down just after John disappeared. John did not reach the house but the family became uneasy and a search was instituted through the lot of the land and killed him instantly.

The death of the boy is a great shock to all the people of the city, most of whom knew him for a long time. He was a native of Dublin and was about 15 years of age, a bright, manly young boy, very popular among his friends. The body will be taken tomorrow to Decatur, where the interment will occur Saturday.

Declaring that it is high time for Georgia to pay its debts, Governor John M. Slaton last night gave out a ringing message to the people dealing with the financial condition of the state.

The only honest way, he urges, is for the state to pay its debts, and under no conditions to spend more than it takes in. He declares that Georgia should set an example for business policy and not permit big processes.

"Certainly the governor," declares Mr. Slaton, "should not be required to draw warrants on a treasury in which there is no money."

Governor Slaton's Message.

Governor Slaton's Message in full is as follows:

"Of course I know the financial state of the situation. Other legislatures have been appaling and this one is called upon to pay up. When the state has no money it is like to spend money, but none of us like the day of settlement. We enjoy living well during the year, but do not like to pay up when the time comes for the reckoning.

"I believe if a man has 15 cents in his pocket he should make his dinner on a sandwich, but he can't have terrapin stew and pie.

"The 1911 the legislature appropriated about $156,000 more than its revenue. In 1912, $427,000; in 1913, $349,000 more than the estimated revenue. These are the legislature figures, making a sum total of $932,000 of appropriations in excess of revenue. This year the general appropriation bill that went to the senate exceeding the anticipated revenue $230,000, making a deficit of $1,215,000, supposing there is no decrease of taxable values.

"It will be thus seen that while the tax limit is 5 mills, the legislature has been appropriating about 6 mills without raising the money. The result of this course is manifest to anybody.

Meaning of the People.

"When the constitutional limitation of 5 mills was adopted nobody supposed the legislature would appropriate in excess of the amount which by that levy. It was a mandate by the people that they only limited such governmental functions, administer schools, pensions or anything else, as

INHERITANCE TAX PASSED BY HOUSE

Swift Substitute Bill Receives an Overwhelming Majority. What the Measure Provides.

The house on Thursday passed the Swift inheritance bill by a vote of 120 to 12.

This measure is a substitute for the three bills introduced by Messrs. Oakes, of Harbor, Ledbetter, of Polk, and Swift, of Muscogee, and was amended by several judiciary committee No. 1.

The bill provides for a levy of a tax upon all real or personal property in the state which shall pass on the death of a decedent by will or by the laws regulating descents and distribution, or by deed, grant or gift, except in case of a bona fide purchase for a full consideration.

A tax of 1 per cent is levied on such property in excess of $5,000 passing to any immediate kin or adopted children of a decedent. A tax of 2 per cent is levied on all property affected by this bill passing to any person, corporation, association other than those included in the 1 per cent class.

This measure, which has been in force in a two states in the union for eighty-five years, and is called in effect in thirty-eight states, is by the vote of the house one of the most popular measures ever passed by the state, and is considered as probably the fairest means of taxation possible.

MAJOR W. W. SCREWS ANSWERS LAST CALL

Veteran Editor of The Montgomery Advertiser Passes Suddenly.

Montgomery, Ala., August 7.—Major William Wallace Screws, editor of The Montgomery Advertiser, died suddenly tonight at his country home at Oakdale, fourteen miles from town, of an attack of acute indigestion. With him at the time of his death were his wife and two of his sons, Benjamin Screws and Stuit Screws.

Major Screws was born February 25, 1839, in Barbour county, Ala. He was without college advantages, but received a good common school education. He studied law and was admitted to the bar in Montgomery before the Civil war. He enlisted early in the struggle and saw service in Texas, Kentucky and Virginia, being captured in the spring of 1865.

He became connected with the Advertiser at the close of the war, and this connection continued until his death. Major Screws served as secretary of state for Alabama from 1878 to 1890, and from 1893 to 1897; he was postmaster at Montgomery. He was president of Alabama Press association, holding the history of Alabama. He was represented next in Masonic circles, and in the Episcopal church. A wife and three sons survive.

Steamer Sinks With Crew.

Valparaiso, Chile, August 7.—The Chi-

basement and killed her there, but at this point, they made a risky decision. They decided to call character witnesses, knowing that once they raised the subject of Leo's character, they would open the door for the prosecution to call witnesses to disparage that character.

It was one thing for a witness to testify that he had seen Leo with Mary or any other girl. The jury could believe him, or they could decide he was lying. It was a different thing—and much more damaging—for a witness or a lawyer to claim that Leo was the sort of man who took advantage of young girls all the time. That type of character attack could only be made after the defense raised the issue of character.

It was a risky strategy. But Arnold and Rosser could see that the technical battle they were winning was not impressing the jury. Perhaps if they could make the jury see Leo through friends and family as a real person, they could win the jury's sympathy and Leo's acquittal.

Several of Leo's friends from Cornell and the Pratt Institute came to Atlanta to testify that Leo's character was excellent. Then John Ashley Jones, the New York Life Insurance Company representative who had insured the superintendent, testified that Leo was not only in excellent physical condition but also that his character was good. That was Dorsey's cue to go on the offensive. In his cross-examination, Dorsey demanded of Jones, "Then you didn't hear that he took girls in his lap down there at the factory?" Although Arnold immediately objected, Judge Roan overruled him on the grounds that the defense had introduced the issue of character, so the prosecution could now challenge the defendant's character.

Dorsey pressed on, asking, "You never heard that Frank went to Druid Hills with a little girl, did you?" and "Didn't you hear about twelve months ago of Frank kissing girls and playing with the nipples of their breasts?"

"No, nor you either," Leo's mother shouted, leaping to her feet and shaking her finger furiously at the solicitor general in outrage. She was escorted out of the courtroom, sobbing, and Dorsey pressed on, voicing every rumor that had flown around Atlanta during the past three and a half months.

Tensions between the prosecution and the defense rose. When Dorsey cross-examined one defense witness on Thursday, August 14, the man interrupted, "Mr. Dorsey, don't twist anything I say." Arnold commented, loudly enough that anyone in the courtroom could hear, "He will anyhow." The two attorneys charged each other and nearly came to blows before they were separated.

Arnold called a number of witnesses who confirmed Leo's timeline of his movements the day Mary was killed. Dorsey tried his best to shake them on their times but was unsuccessful. Then Arnold brought in another group of character witnesses, ranging from factory workers and members of Atlanta's Jewish community to more old friends from Cornell. The *Constitution* reported, "The sordid surroundings lost some of their grimness as witness and prisoner gripped hands silently or spoke the few simple words of greeting."

Then they called Leo's mother to the stand, hoping to crush the image of the Franks as wealthy Jews. She explained that they had no

Rachel (Rae) Frank, Leo Frank's mother, took the stand in her son's defense, a move that probably hurt the defense more than helped.

estate, had a mortgage on their ten-thousand-dollar home, and lived on the interest income from twenty thousand dollars. While that didn't sound like a wealthy estate to a New Yorker, it sounded like considerable wealth to the poor workers of Atlanta in the crowd and to many of the jurors.

The defense rested with Leo Frank on Monday afternoon. In 1913 Georgia, the accused could not give sworn testimony and be cross-examined, but he could speak to the court. Leo did so for four hours. His intention was to speak calmly and reasonably, giving the jury the facts of the case as dispassionately as he could. To help jurors see how seriously he took his work in the factory, Leo brought in a display showing the variety of pencils the National Pencil Company manufactured. However, Dorsey objected on the grounds that the pencil display had not been introduced as evidence. Leo went on to try to describe his work without his visual aids.

Puzzled by his careful discussion of pencil production and unmoved by his fascination with the details of the invoicing report he had been preparing on April 26, the jury waited to hear Leo sound as passionate as Jim Conley. They were stunned that he had so little to say about Mary Phagan—even though Leo felt he could not have said more since he hadn't known the girl and had only seen her briefly on the day she died.

But in the end, Leo found the eloquence the jury had been waiting to hear:

> *The statement of the negro Conley is a tissue of lies from first to last. I know nothing whatever of the cause of the death of Mary Phagan and Conley's statement as to his coming up and helping me dispose of the body, or that I had anything to do with her or to do with him that day is a monstrous lie. . . .*
>
> *The story as to women coming into the factory with me for immoral purposes is a base lie and the few occasions that he claims to have seen me in indecent positions with women is a lie so vile that I have no language with which to fitly denounce it. . . .*

THE STANDARD SOUTHERN NEWSPAPER

THE ATLANTA CONSTITUTION

THE STANDARD SOUTHERN NEWSPAPER

Vol. XLVI—No. 64.

ATLANTA, GA. TUESDAY MORNING, AUGUST 19, 1913.—FOURTEEN PAGES.

Daily and Sunday, carrier delivery, 12 cents weekly.
Single copies on the streets and at newsstands, 5 cents.

FRANK ENDS STATEMENT AFTER TESTIFYING FOUR HOURS

"Silent Man in Tower" Tells His Story to Men Who Will Decide His Fate

Two poses of Leo M. Frank on the witness stand on Monday afternoon telling his story to the jury. In one picture he is shown with his notes in his hand.

Frank on the stand was cool, perfectly poised and at all times the master of himself. He showed no trace of nervousness. He looked the jury squarely in the face. He was at times explicit when explaining the details of his business, argumentative when telling of things that had looked dark for him, eloquent as he concluded.

"I'VE TOLD THE WHOLE TRUTH" SAYS PRISONER CONCLUDING DRAMATIC STORY TO THE JURY

Discussing Much-Fought-Over Point of His Alleged Nervousness on the Morning of the Murder, Superintendent Admits It Freely, Declaring That Any Man in His Place Would Have Been Similarly Affected—Speaks Bitterly of His Treatment by Members of Detective Force, and Says That One Reason Why He Would Not Consent to Meet Conley Was That the Officers Would Have Distorted His Words.

MOTHER AND WIFE OF DEFENDANT EMBRACE HIM WHEN HE LEAVES STAND

Declares Story of Conley Was a Lie From Beginning to End, and Denies Charge of Miss Jackson That He Ever Looked Into Dressing Room of Girl Employees—He Tells of Mary Phagan Coming to Office to Get Her Pay Envelope Shortly After Noon on April 26. Says That He Gave Detectives Clue That Conley Could Write, Which Led to Arrest of Negro Sweeper—No Fund Raised for His Defense, He Asserts.

"Some newspaper man has called me 'The Silent Man in the Tower.' Gentlemen, this is the time and here is the place." I have told you the truth, the whole truth and nothing but the truth."

Thus did Leo M. Frank dramatically conclude his remarkable statement of nearly four hours, during which time he was in turn explicit as to detail of his doings on the day of the murder, argumentative when explaining some point which had looked dark for him, tender when referring to his wife and his home life, bitter when he told of the treatment he had received at the hands of the detective department.

It was in all essentials the most remarkable statement which has ever been delivered in a courtroom in the south. Through the four hours that he was talking there was not the slightest trace of nervousness, not a tremor of the hands, even when conveying a glass of water to his lips. He was perfectly poised, convincingly clear in his statement, the man unafraid.

When he concluded a hush fell over the courtroom. His wife and mother, who had been hanging on his every word, fell forward on his neck and the gentlemen tears flowed freely.

The statement carried the ring of truth in every sentence, and scores in the room whose minds had not been made up left the room convinced of the man's innocence.

FRANK THE MASTER OF HIMSELF.

Shortly before court convened for the afternoon session Frank was chatting with his wife and some friends in the ante-room. He had just had his throat treated for an extremely bad cold which he contracted some days ago. With this exception he stated to a newspaper man that he was feeling fine—that he felt no nervousness, and that he expected to be on the stand fully three hours.

Shortly after 2 o'clock Frank took the stand. The courtroom was packed. Scores of citizens crowded near. His devoted mother and his faithful wife, her sisters and cousins, sat where they could see him clearly.

He began his statement with a swift account of his life and then hurried forward to the events of the fatal day when Mary Phagan entered the office of the National Pencil company for the last time.

He told in detail of his movements and activities that day. From time to time he referred to the financial statement and to various papers on which he says he worked that day. These papers he went over carefully, item by item, figure by figure. He stood facing the jury and talked to them very much as if he were addressing a board of directors before whom he was presenting some proposition demanding explanation.

For some two hours he dwelt on the technical details of the factory to show just how much time it would have taken him to make up the financial statement, and he explained in minute fashion the source from which each item was derived.

LOST SIGHT OF MARY PHAGAN.

He told of little Mary Phagan entering his office to receive her pay, of her going out and then returning to inquire if the metal had come. As she left for the last time he spoke of having heard what he thought was a woman's voice, but of this he said he could not be positive.

He visualized for the jury his work of that afternoon and of his trip to and from home; of how he spent Saturday evening.

Of the early morning ride to the undertaking establishment and of his alleged nervousness he said:

"A good deal has been said of my nervousness that morning. I admit it. I was nervous. Think of it, gentlemen. I was awakened at an early hour, rushed downtown in an automobile going at top speed. I had had no breakfast. I witnessed this poor child—this young girl in the first flush of womanhood—dead and mutilated. Gentlemen, the sight was enough to make any man nervous. It would have touched any man not made of stone."

Frank then told of his visit to the detective department and of his second visit to the undertaking establishment that afternoon.

Of his experience with the Atlanta detective department he spoke with a trace of bitterness.

He described the manner in which he says John Black administered the third degree to Newt Lee. He said the manner in which he shrieked at and cursed the negro was something awful.

Of the criticism that he would not talk to detectives or to Conley, he said:

"My experience with them showed me that they would put words in my mouth and distort what I really said until it became unrecognizable. At first I answered all questions gladly, but finally I decided to have no hands of them."

He told of a visit from John Black and Harry Scott and how they had placed him...

NO TRACE FOUND OF FLEEING THAW BY HIS PURSUERS

Warrants Issued for Five Men Who Aided Slayer of Stanford White to Escape from Matteawan.

New York, August 18.—Sundown tonight marked the thirty-sixth hour of Harry K. Thaw's freedom and the defiee of the United States and Canada had not picked up his trail. The week list now as the slayer of Stanford White, or as escaped lunatic, but on a warrant issued at Poughkeepsie today charging him with conspiring with the aged keeper, Howard Barnum, and the five men who managed the asylum delivery.

On such a technicality does New York state base its hope of bringing about the fugitive's return. Both factions of the double-barreled government at Albany have promised rigid investigation and the exertion of every effort to bring about his capture.

Thaw's seclusion today and tonight was absolute. Out of the cloud of dust which settled in the wake of the black automobile bearing him and his liberators from Matteawan Sunday morning nothing tangible had come except a historic letter from Thaw himself assuring his aged mother in New York that he desired rest and would in due time join her at the Thaw country place, Elmhurst, at Cresson, Penn., in obedi...

Continued on Page Three.

The Men Who Fill Prescriptions

Must know their business to a "T," or they're liable to bring disaster on a druggist.

Competent drug clerks, as well as other kinds of skilled men, may be quickly reached through a Constitution Want Ad.

They read this paper every morning. Whom they are out of a job or looking for a better one, it is quite natural that they should read the Want Ads—and then use them.

HUERTA ULTIMATUM TO UNITED STATES; IMMEDIATE RECOGNITION IS DEMANDED

MEMBERS OF MOB SHOT BY SHERIFF

Brave Officer and One Deputy Repulses the Would-Be Lynchers as They Storm Jail at Spartanburg.

Spartanburg, S. C., August 18.—Three men were wounded here tonight when a mob stormed the county jail in an effort to lynch Will Fair, a negro criminally assaulted an aged woman near here today.
Are Frank Epples, John Throne.
Sheriff White pluckily repulsed...

Continued on...

United States Given Till Midnight to Answer—Failure to Comply Means That Huerta Will Sever All Relations With This Country—All American Proposals Spurned.

Mexico City, August 18.—The United States government has been given until midnight tonight by President Huerta to recognize Mexico, it is officially stated.

The government is not specific in the public announcement as to what course them will be pursued but it is understood that it means the severing of all relations between the two countries.

Senor Urrutia, minister of the interior, who on previous occasions has been spokesman for the administration, was the person chosen tonight to make the announcement.

NEWS PUZZLING TO WASHINGTON

Bryan Denies Huerta Ultimatum Has Been Received. Admits Huerta Has Rejected American Proposals.

Washington, August 18.—Administration officials were puzzled tonight when they received the announcement through press dispatches that President Huerta had delivered an ultimatum demanding...

col. 2

Gentlemen, some newspaper men have called me "the silent man in the tower," and I have kept my silence and my counsel advisedly, until the proper time and place. The time is now; the place is here; and I have told you the truth, the whole truth.

Many people in the courtroom were moved by Leo's closing, but easily as many were chilled by the earlier part of his statement and by the fact that he was more excited by pencil manufacture than by the death of one of his workers.

After the defense rested, the prosecution had the opportunity to call rebuttal witnesses. Dorsey called a group of factory girls to challenge Leo's character with further claims of sexual impropriety. Rosser was careful in his cross-examination, not wanting to appear to bully the girls. He even chose not to cross-examine some of them. To the jury, that suggested the defense accepted the girls' testimony as truth, and Dorsey emphasized that interpretation in his closing argument, crying, "They didn't dare to do it."

Arnold and Rosser each spoke in closing arguments for the defense, and each was effective in tearing apart Dorsey's web of circumstantial evidence. Arnold clearly pointed out the errors in Jim Conley's testimony and showed how the defense had refuted the other prosecution witnesses. He contended that Dorsey "almost changed the course of time in an effort to get Frank convicted," and closed by telling the jury that the state's case was built solely on "prejudice and perjury. I have never seen such malice, such personal hatred in all my life."

Rosser attacked the investigation, detailing how police had browbeaten their witnesses. He concluded by attacking the prosecution for teaching Jim Conley the story to tell in court and calling the man "a trained parrot." He closed by saying, "I don't believe any man, no matter what his race, ought to be tried under such testimony. I might [hang a man on such testimony] in the daytime, but at night when things got quiet I would be ashamed of myself."

Hugh Dorsey's closing argument for the prosecution was masterful. He spoke for nine hours over three days, presenting Jim Conley as a simple worker who had admitted to being paid off by a powerful white

Jew to help hide his boss's crime. Dorsey praised the workers and the good country people who had come forward to denounce the fiend. At the end, he turned to Leo and attacked him directly:

"You assaulted her, and she resisted. She wouldn't yield. You struck her and you ravished her and she was unconscious."

Mary's mother was seated at the prosecution table with her other daughter, and when she heard this, she screamed and buried her face in the girl's arms. Dorsey continued:

"You tell me she wasn't ravished? I ask you to look at the blood—you tell me that little child wasn't ravished? I ask you to look at the drawers, that were torn. I ask you to look at the blood on the drawers. . . . "

Lucille, seated just behind Leo, sobbed. Dorsey faced her husband and said:

> You gagged her, and then quickly you tipped up to the front, where you knew there was a cord, and you got the cord and in order to save your reputation which you had among the members of the B'nai B'rith, in order to save, not your character, because you never had it, but in order to save the reputation with [the Jewish community] and your kinfolks in Brooklyn, rich and poor, and in Athens, then it was that you got the cord and fixed the little girl whom you'd assaulted, who wouldn't yield to your proposals, to save your reputation, because dead people tell no tales.

Dorsey completed his closing argument on Monday, August 25, his voice hoarse and tiring as he told the jury that Mary Phagan

> died a noble death, not a blot on her name. She died because she wouldn't yield her virtue to the demands of her superintendent.
>
> Your Honor, I have done my duty. . . . And I predict, may it please Your Honor, that under the law that you give in charge and under the honest opinion of the jury of the evidence produced, there can be but one verdict, and that is: We the jury find the defendant, Leo M. Frank, guilty!

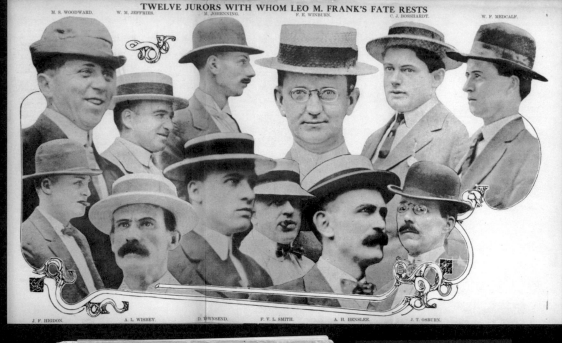

TWELVE JURORS WITH WHOM LEO M. FRANK'S FATE RESTS

M. S. WOODWARD. W. M. JEFFRIES. M. JOHENNING. F. E. WINBURN. C. J. BOSSHARDT. W. F. MEDCALF.

J. F. HIGDON. A. L. WISBEY. D. TOWNSEND. F. V. L. SMITH. A. H. HENSLEE. J. T. OSBURN.

ARGUMENT OF
HUGH M. DORSEY
Solicitor-General, Atlanta Judicial Circuit

AT THE TRIAL OF

LEO M. FRANK
Charged with the murder of Mary Phagan

Published by
N. CHRISTOPHULOS,
411 Third Street
Macon, Ga.

Above: A newspaper photo of the members of the Leo Frank jury.

Left: Hugh Dorsey's closing argument in the case lasted nine hours. It was published as a book the following year.

Hugh Dorsey had timed it perfectly. As he spoke the word *guilty*, nearby church bells rang out the noon hour. Dorsey repeated, "Guilty! Guilty! Guilty!" as the twelve chimes sounded, each chime a "guilty" charge for each juror who was about to retire to consider his verdict.

The jury left the old city hall for lunch, walking through the streets packed with a crowd of five thousand people demanding Leo Frank's blood. When they returned from their meal, the jury took only an hour and forty-five minutes and two ballots to reach a verdict. Fearful that mob violence would break out, Judge Roan cleared the courtroom. He also asked that Leo and his attorneys not be present when the verdict was read. Although this technically denied the accused due process of law, the judge feared that Leo and his lawyers would be in physical danger if the jury acquitted him, and Rosser and Arnold agreed to the request.

Jury foreman Fred Winburn faced the judge with only Hugh Dorsey in the courtroom and announced, his voice unsteady, that Leo Frank was found guilty of the murder of Mary Phagan.

When he received the news, Leo gasped, "My God! Even the jury was influenced by mob law. I am as innocent as I was a year ago." Lucille sobbed bitterly. The *Constitution* reported she "cuddled closer to her boyish-looking husband. . . . He stroked her head and pleaded with her to be brave." No one other than Leo and Lucille's immediate family knew at this time that Lucille had miscarried and lost their child. She must have thought at this moment that she was about to lose her husband and any chance for their future children, as well.

Hugh Dorsey came out of the building and only walked a few steps before members of the crowd hoisted him to their shoulders and carried him, cheering loudly. The following week, Dorsey was the guest of honor at a celebration barbecue that also paid tribute to all twelve members of the jury in attendance.

Jim Conley would be found guilty of accessory after the fact to Mary Phagan's murder and would be sentenced to serve one year on the chain gang. But Leo Frank was sentenced to be hanged on October 10, 1913.

THE STANDARD SOUTHERN NEWSPAPER

THE ATLANTA CONSTITUTION

THE STANDARD SOUTHERN NEWSPAPER

Vol. XLVI—No. 71.　　ATLANTA, GA. TUESDAY MORNING, AUGUST 26, 1913.—SIXTEEN PAGES.　　Daily and Sunday, carrier delivery, 12 cents weekly.
Single copies on the streets and at newsstands, 5 cents.

FRANK CONVICTED, ASSERTS INNOCENCE

LIND QUITS MEXICO; WILSON'S MESSAGE GOES TO CONGRESS

The President Will Personally Present Views on Situation to Joint Session of House and Senate.

CONFERENCE IS HELD AT THE WHITE HOUSE

Wilson Reads Message to Two Congressional Foreign Relations Committees and It Is Given Approval.

Mexico City, August 25.—President Wilson's personal representative, John Lind, will leave the Mexican capital tomorrow, proceeding to Vera Cruz.

Mr. Lind called on Foreign Minister Gamboa today to say good-bye, but there was nothing in their conversation regarding the resumption of negotiations as to indicate that Mexico would recede from her position.

Mr. Lind will sail from Vera Cruz at an early date, presumably on a battleship. It is expected that William Bayard Hale, who has been in Mexico City in an official capacity, will accompany Mr. Lind or leave soon afterward.

Huerta Calling Army Officers.

Rumors persist that General Treviño, who has been summoned to the capital, will become provisional president, but confirmation is lacking and the report to affect to another that General Huerta has called to most of the retired officers and many of those on detached service to report for duty.

General Felix Diaz, who started for Japan as special Mexican ambassador, also is said to have received a summons to return to the capital.

Mexicans and foreign residents manifest great uneasiness at present over the developments in the Mexican situation through the transmission of President Wilson's message to congress, but the government in announcement and will maintain its reserve until after the message has been read.

MESSAGE ON MEXICO READ TO CONGRESSMEN

Washington, August 25.—President Wilson will read his message on the Mexican situation at the noon session tomorrow. This was decided at midnight, following the receipt of a message from John Lind, personal representative of President Wilson in Mexico, that he had sold good-bye to Foreign Minister Gamboa, and would leave Mexico City tomorrow. Negotiations, so far as Mr. Lind is concerned, have been terminated. The United States will receive any further proposals through Charge d'affaires O'Shaughnessy, at the American embassy.

The policy of the United States was submitted to the members of the two congressional committees of foreign relations today at a conference at the white house by President Wilson and Secretary Bryan. The president's message received practically unanimous approval. The fullest course of this government will be one of non-interference, in the hope that the effect of the present efforts and the presence of foreign governments will constitute a moral suasion that ultimately will bring about peace in Mexico.

The message makes it plain—that there will be no lifting of the embargo on arms, that no faction or government in Mexico will be allowed to receive munitions of war from the United States. If necessary the president proposes to increase the American border patrol to safeguard the public.

Wilson Cites Precedent.

The president cites in his message, as a precedent for the policy he proposes to pursue, an action of President Harrison in withholding recognition from (five for more than a year after the latter had gained control of the Mexican government.

During today's conference, the president referred to the committees not only the full text of his own message but the action exchanged between John Lind and Huerta.

President Wilson's message is one of friendship, not of hostility, and precedes a policy of absolute non-interference. It proclaims to the

Continued on Last Page.

Traveling Salesmen Who Sell the Goods

Men of experience and enthusiasm who can hold down expenses and increase sales may be quickly reached with a Constitution Want Ad.

Business will boom this fall. Now's the time to whip your sales force into shape. Phone Main 5000 of Atlanta 100 and ask for an ad taker.

First thing every morning men who are out of work or want better jobs read the Want Ads in The Constitution.

Index to Want Ads Page 12 Col. 2

"You Can't" Cannot Provide for Nothing."

THE ATLANTA CONSTITUTION

FARM CURRENCY WINS IN CAUCUS

Paper Based on Agricultural Products on the Same Basis as Commercial Paper for Banking Purposes.

Washington, August 25.—An agricultural currency amendment to the administration currency bill was adopted by the house democratic caucus tonight. After several preliminary skirmishes, in which other amendments were beaten the caucus, without a dissenting vote, adopted an amendment agreed to both by the "insurgent" contingent and banking and currency committee to put paper based on agricultural products on the same basis as commercial paper for banking purposes.

It also would extend the maturity of notes and bills allotted to discount under the amendment to ninety days instead of the originally proposed sixty days. This action disposes of the last of the big controversial ones in the administration currency bill.

Text of the Amendment.

The amendment, the result of many conferences and concurred in by administration leaders and those unsuccessfully seeking other amendments, reads:

"Upon the indorsement of any member bank, any federal reserve bank may discount notes and bills of exchange arising out of commercial transactions, that is, notes and bills of exchange issued or drawn for agricultural, industrial or commercial purposes or the proceeds of which have been used or may be used for such purposes the federal reserve board to have the right to determine or define the character of the paper thus eligible for discount, within the meaning of this act. But such definition shall not include notes or bills issued or drawn for the purpose of carrying or trading in stocks, bonds or other investment securities, except bonds and notes of the government of the United States. Nothing herein contained shall be construed to prohibit such notes and bills of exchange, secured by staple agricultural products or other goods, wares or merchandise from being eligible for such discount.

"Notes and bills admitted to discount under the terms of this paragraph must have a maturity of not more than ninety days.

"We have seen all we intended for," was the comment of Representative Neeley, of Kansas, in charge of the opposition to the bill.

"The Glass amendment," added Representative Henry, of Texas, "means months."

Sam Henry Surrendered.

"To-the-s decisive section as thus amended," replied Chairman Glass, "does just that we have wanted all along. On one of the wild and absurd arguments which have been proposed we have struggled along and simply hammered along and simply allowed him to our beaten. He pressed after the boat left the wharf."

Other members of the committee made similar statements.

Chairman Glass said tonight that the amendment did not discriminate either for against the farmer; that the New England shoe manufacturer or small trader could present his wares for discount as much as the southern cotton farmer. He took the position "in whose thing is left to the federal reserve board of the regional reserve bank which does the discounting."

During today's caucus the caucus defeated an amendment by Representative Wilson, of Arkansas, to exclude from rediscounting at federal reserve banks, notes or bills intended for dealing in futures or the marginal trading of agricultural products. Representative Glass, of Indiana, in the printing speech of the day, ineffectually sought to divide the federal reserve districts into four geographical divisions.

Weather Prophecy
CLEAR.

GEORGIA—Generally fair Tuesday and Wednesday.

Local Report.

Lowest temperature 66
Highest temperature 87
Mean temperature 76
Normal temperature 79
Rainfall in past 24 hours, .0 inch.
Deficiency since 1st of month, in. 1.05
Deficiency since January 1, in. 1.14

Reports From Various Stations.

BETS ON HORSE RACES BY HIGH U. S. OFFICIALS

Washington, August 25.—Nineteen have been having fun betting on horse races, according to the police, has not been confined to the clerks in the government departments, but that certain high officials also were arrested in the race today. The investigation declared today, the "men higher up" made their wagers through outside ones, and as a result their exposure was, it is declared.

The country to the basketball betting industry in the departments, the police say, has led them to discover that a very large percentage of the gamblers with resources of upward of a half million dollars. Fourteen years it is said, the "ring" divided their profits annually ranging into the thousands of dollars.

NEGRO SHOT TO DEATH BY A "TARHEEL" MOB

Charlotte, N. C., August 25.—Joe McNeely, a negro, who shot and mortally wounded policeman L. L. Wilson, Friday, was taken from the Good Samaritan hospital at an early hour this morning and shot to death by a mob of several hundred men.

ATTENDANCE MARK SOUGHT BY LOCALS

Want 200,000 for the Season. "Birmingham Must Be Beaten," Is Slogan—Field Day Wednesday.

As the Southern league teams come thundering down the stretch, with the Crackers having a chance to overtake the Middle Cubs and win the third pennant for the Gate City of the South, the attendance proposition opens here the discussion.

Atlanta must beat Mobile (on the percentage basis). Birmingham must be beaten for the attendance honor. At present, the Gual Baroom are leading the Crackers by a couple of thousand paid attendance for the season.

The season record of paid attendance now held by Atlanta, 198,800. Those local clubs hope to surpass this figure this season. Two hundred thousand and Birmingham must be beaten" is the season slogan.

With the completing the argument of such an interesting point, the attendance should be "large for the Birmingham to again challenge its legs right to be called the best ball team in the Southern league has awakened an enthusiastic shift to the present scrap.

Merchants Behind Move.

The local merchants are lined up behind the full club in their endeavor to establish an astonishing record that will require considerable effort to pass in years to come.

First, several merchants have agreed to present prizes to the members of the Atlanta and Memphis teams for a field day which will be held Wednesday. This being a half holiday for the grocers and furniture, a great crowd is sure to be on hand to witness the field sports and the ball game.

Five events will be contested. Here are the events and the prizes that will be donated to the winners in each event:

100-yard Dash—Hat, Law Bros. 50-yard Dash—$5.
Circling the Bases—Pair of shoes, Nick Bros.
Fungo Hitting—Two silk shirts, Parks-Chambers-Hardwick company.
Long-distance Throwing—Silk umbrella, George Muse Clothing company.

To help tell this man in bolstering the attendance locally the following merchants have agreed to allow their employees as many days off the number of the season as will be consistent with the maintenance of their business.

W. s. Chapin Insurance company; Royal Insurance company; Georgia Railway and power company, Southern Bell Telephone and Telegraph company; Third National bank, Lowry National bank, V. H. Kriegshaber & Son, and there are others that will be announced tomorrow.

Atlanta is baseball mad. Local fans want Atlanta to win the pennant. Local business men want them to have the largest attendance and these prizes that Atlanta is the best baseball city in the south.

The Atlanta spirit is working overtime.

CONSTITUTION'S EXTRA TELLS ATLANTA OF THE VERDICT IN FRANK CASE

Within three minutes after Foreman Fred Winburn had announced the verdict of guilty in the Frank case, The Constitution's extra, giving full details of incidents in the courtroom during the entire time the jury was deliberating, and all exclusive facts after that dramatic moment, was on the streets.

It was conceded that The Constitution's extra was the most complete issue of the day. Not only did it flash to the anxious readers of Atlanta the first news that Frank had been doomed, but it also went to the suburban districts and out on every train leaving the city.

This piece of enterprise was made possible by having a corps of well-trained newspaper men on the scene, and having every arrangement made beforehand to cover the verdict without the waste of a single second.

It will be remembered that the news of the tragic death of Mary Phagan was first told to the people of the city by an extra issued by The Constitution on the morning of April 27, within a short time after the body was found in the basement of the National Pencil company.

GUILTY, DECLARES JURY

LEO M. FRANK.

LEO FRANK'S LIFE HISTORY.

The following chronological history of the life of Leo M. Frank is taken from his statement to the jury, made August 18:

April 17, 1884, born in Paris, Texas.
July, 1884, taken by parents to live in Brooklyn, N. Y.
June, 1902, graduated from Pratt institute, a Brooklyn high school.
September, 1902, entered Cornell university, Ithaca, N. Y.
June, 1906, graduated from Cornell.
July, 1906, accepted position as draftsman with B. F. Sturtevant company, of High Park, Mass.
January, 1907, became testing engineer and draftsman for the National Meter company, of Brooklyn.
October, 1907, came to Atlanta to confer with friends here about establishment of a pencil company.
December, 1907, went to Europe to study the pencil business.
August, 1908, returned from Europe and came directly to Atlanta, where he has remained ever since, as superintendent of the National Pencil factory.
October, 1910, married to Miss Lucile Selig, daughter of Mr. and Mrs. Emil Selig, and went to live with his wife's parents at 68 East Georgia avenue.
April 26, 1913, paid of Mary Phagan at the factory office.
April 27, 1913, notified early in the morning by officers to come to his factory. Visited morgue and saw the girl's body and then went to factory.
April 29, 1913, gives first statement to detectives at police station.
April 29, 1913, arrested on suspicion of the crime.
May 1, 1913, bound over by the coroner's jury on charge of murder of Mary Phagan and taken to the Tower.
May 24, 1913, indicted by the Fulton grand jury for the murder.
July 28, 1913, his trial begins.
August 18, 1913, makes statement to jury.
August 25, 1913, found guilty.

Friends Tell Frank in Tower Of Jury's Verdict of Guilty; Prisoner Cheers Weeping Wife

It was exactly 5:30 o'clock before Frank knew of the jury's verdict.

Seated in his quarters in the Tower, the prisoner and his wife chatted of things to come in the future. They both smiling and appeared happy at the apparent thought that the setting sun would bring him freedom.

In the office of Sheriff Mangum located on the first floor of the Tower, Rabbi Marx and a group of staunch friends of the accused debated as to whom would bring the message and shatter the one remaining ray of hope they had buoyed up in the prisoner.

Finally, clustering the group of Frank, including Dr. Rosenberg, the family physician, were summoned and the telephone and asked to hasten to the prison and convey the news to the prisoner. A great crowd gathered in front of the Tower, but it was quietly gathering composed for the most part of newly men and women who had gathered at the prison gate to catch a glimpse of the prisoner as he went from and returned to the jail after an all-day grind.

Dr. Rosenberg Arrives.

Just a few minutes after 5:30 Dr. Rosenberg, the Frank family physician, arrived at the jail. He was

proceeded to convey the news to the prisoner and his wife.

Frank was seated at the right side of his wife. They were both smiling. Around them grouped were friends. Intuition probably told them that sad news was coming, for on the faces of each one disappointment and sorrow could be read. As Rabbi Marx, his breast closely to Doctor Rosenberg, entered the cell, Frank left his seat to greet them. If he anticipated any news he did not betray it in his greeting.

"I can glad you come up," Frank assured his family physician.

Rabbi Marx, solemn and dejected, moved to where Dr. R. Wildauer and other friends were seated. There were traces of tears in his eyes.

"Leo, the jury has found you guilty," Dr. Rosenberg said.

Informed by Man Laws.

The silence was dreadful. Mrs. Frank cuddled closer to her husband, looking bushland. There was a wild stare in her eyes. No one in the cell seemed to grasp the meaning of the fatal pronouncement. Only Frank seemed to be composed.

"My God! Even the jury was influenced by mob law."

Continued on Page Seven.

WAITS WITH WIFE IN TOWER FOR NEWS FROM COURTROOM; FRIENDS TELL HIM VERDICT

"I Am as Innocent Today as I Was One Year Ago," He Cries—"The Jury Has Been Influenced by Mob Law"—"I Am Stunned by News," Declares Rabbi Marx, One of Prisoner's Closest Friends—Defense Plans to Carry Case to Supreme Court in Order to Secure New Trial—Judge Roan Will Defer Sentence For a Few Days.

OVATION FOR JURY AND SOLICITOR GIVEN BY CROWD WAITING ON STREET

Judge Roan Thanks Jurymen for Services During Four Long, Hard Weeks, and Tells Members He Hopes They Will Find Their Families Well—Courtroom Was Cleared by Order of Judge Before Jury Was Brought in to Give Its Verdict—"I'm Sorry for Frank's Wife and His Mother," Says Solicitor Dorsey.

Leo M. Frank, superintendent of the National Pencil factory; president of the B'nai B'rith, graduate of Cornell university, student of literature, and until recently regarded as a man of unblemished character and reputation, and a leader among his people, has been declared guilty of the murder of Mary Phagan, a 13-year-old employee of the factory of which Frank is the head.

At a minutes to 5 o'clock a jury of his peers filed slowly into the courtroom, which for four weeks has been the scene of the greatest legal battle in the history of the state.

The room had been cleared of the morbidly curious who for days have listened to the fierce fight for and against the young man. Only the newspapermen, Sheriff Mangum, his deputies, Solicitor Dorsey and Frank Hooper, a few lawyers and some close personal friends of the defendant were in the room.

VERDICT WAS EASY TO READ.

On the face of each juror was the drawn look of men who had been compelled, through duty, to do an awful thing—to consign a fellow creature to the gallows. There was no mistaking that look. The strongest of the men shook as if some strange ailment had stricken them.

It took no student of human nature to read that the verdict was the ultimate one of guilt.

A hush fell over the courtroom. The scraping of a chair across the floor, the rustle of a fan, the shuffling of a foot would have been welcome sounds. The silence was fearsome.

Slowly, with voice that trembled, Fred Winburn, foreman of the jury, read the verdict.

Immediately there was the hustle and bustle of reporters and strident voices calling out "guilty" over the telephones to Atlanta's three newspapers.

The sound reached the street below and a shout went up from the waiting mob outside.

The end had come to the longest criminal trial on record in this state.

JUDGE THANKS THE JURY.

Just after the ballot was polled Judge Roan said:

"Gentlemen, I am now taking leave of you. You have been here for a month, and it has been a hard and trying time for all of us.

"Gentlemen, I want to thank you for your faithful service and consideration of all details in this most arduous case."

The judge's voice broke at this point, but bravely collecting his composure, he continued:

"Gentlemen, I hope you find your families well."

Frank was not in the courtroom.

Luther Rosser, Reuben Arnold and Herbert Haas, attorneys for the defense, were not present when the verdict was read. Each was in his residence, recuperating from the weeks of terrific strain undergone in their masterful fight. They were represented by Stiles Hopkins, a member of Rosser's firm, and Luther Z. Rosser, Jr., son of the attorney.

The verdict was reached at 3:39 o'clock and was read in court at 4:56 o'clock.

FRANK HEARS FATE IN TOWER.

In the Tower, oblivious of his fate, sat Leo M. Frank, his arm around his faithful wife. His presence in court had been waived.

When, some three-quarters of an hour later, he learned the news, he bore up with fortitude. To a friend he said:

"My God! Even the jury was influenced by mob law."

"I am as innocent as I was one year ago."

His wife swooned away when she heard the awful news.

Judge Roan will not pass the death sentence on Frank for some days. He has not definitely decided when.

Attorneys Arnold and Rosser will make a motion for a new

Continued on Page Four.

"THE ASSENT OF A TERRORIZED JURY"

A NEW TRIAL?

Leo wrote from prison to John Gould, a classmate from Cornell, "In April 1913, outrageous trouble overtook me like a bolt from the blue. The charge was so preposterous that at first I treated the matter disdainfully, it was all so foreign and far removed from my most fantastic conception of thought." Now that he had been convicted of murder, Leo was treating the matter very seriously indeed. Leo, Lucille, and his lawyers worked together to plan a course of action to either get a new trial or to reverse the jury's decision.

Despite the urgency of the situation, Rosser and Arnold agreed to a request from the prosecution not to appeal on the grounds that Leo wasn't in court when the verdict was read. The attorneys were confident that they had more than enough grounds for appeal without this one. Why they agreed to anything Hugh Dorsey asked, however, has mystified legal scholars.

In 1913 Georgia, a capital murder case could only be appealed based on errors in law and the motion for appeal had to go to the original judge who had presided over the trial. Rosser and Arnold found over one hundred points of law to appeal, including their argument that Conley's testimony should have been ruled inadmissible, the crowd's influence on the jury, and charges that several jurors were anti-Semitic and had lied to get on the jury in order to convict Frank. Although the appeal delayed Leo's execution,

Judge Roan denied the motion for a new trial on October 31, stating that the legal issues were clear. He admitted, "With all the thought I have put on this case, I am not thoroughly convinced that Frank is guilty or innocent." But Roan then stated, "The jury was convinced. There is no room to doubt that. I feel it is my duty to order that the motion for a new trial be overruled."

Rosser announced that they would appeal to the Georgia Supreme Court on the basis of Judge Roan's admission of doubt. Leo waited in prison for their decision, but on February 17, 1914, the Georgia Supreme Court justices ruled 4–2 that the trial judge was the only one who could decide whether or not the crowd had prevented a fair trial. They stated that Judge Roan's admission of doubt wasn't enough to make them overturn the verdict.

At the hearing to set a new date for execution, Leo again insisted that he was innocent, blaming his conviction on rumors instead of facts. "Not only were these stories circulated in the street, but to the shame of our community be it said that these vile insinuations crept into my very trial in the courtroom, creeping in insidiously, like a thief in the night. The virus of these damning insinuations entered the minds of the twelve men and stole away their judicial frame of mind and their moral courage." Leo's new date of execution was set for April 17, 1914—his thirtieth birthday.

Leo decided that his lawyers had not been serving him well and hired new attorneys. The cost of his defense was mounting far beyond what he and the owners of the National Pencil Company could afford. But word of his case had reached the ears of the American Jewish Committee by means of letters and a series of seven leaflets that Leo handwrote in his cell and then gave to Lucille to type for him. The leaflets explored the contradictions in the solicitor general's case and showed the impossibility of reconciling Conley's story with the nineteen other timeline witnesses, whose testimony fit "together like pieces of mosaic." Of those nineteen witnesses, only ten were for the defense—the other nine were the State of Georgia's own witnesses. Leo urged readers, "Think it over, there is no excuse for a mistake to be made, with open eyes, by an individual or a community."

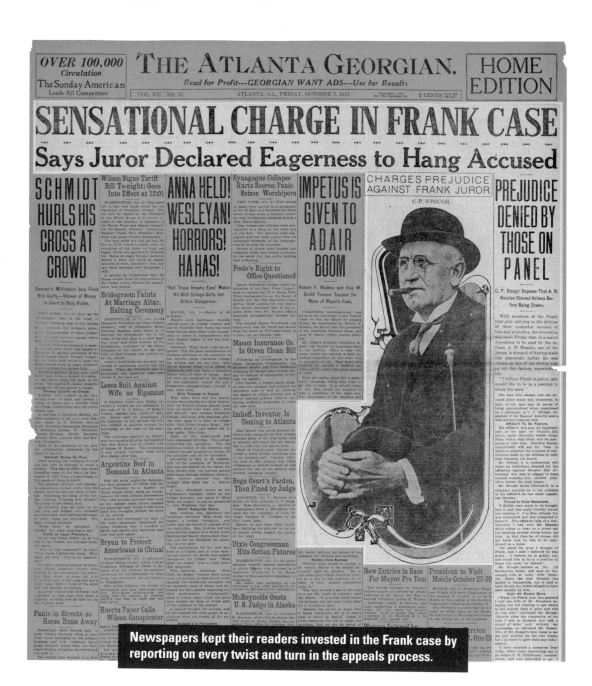

Newspapers kept their readers invested in the Frank case by reporting on every twist and turn in the appeals process.

When renowned constitutional lawyer Louis Marshall, the American Jewish Committee's president, read Leo's leaflets and the letters from Atlanta Jews and other Jews across the country, he realized two things. Public opinion had to be shifted in the southern press, and Leo needed a legal fund to pay his lawyers and pay for press liaison work. Accordingly, the committee worked to raise money from philanthropists, most of them Jewish, such as Chicago advertising magnate Albert Lasker.

Lasker neglected his own business to personally direct new investigators and detectives and to help advise Leo's attorneys. According to Lasker's biographer, John Gunther, "Every instinct he had for justice and fair play, for racial tolerance, for dignity in the courts and good citizenship, was aroused."

The first thing Leo's new team did was make two motions before the Fulton County Superior Court in April 1914. One was an appeal on the basis that Leo had been denied due process of law because he was not permitted to be present in court when the verdict was read. They felt the promise the other attorneys had made to Dorsey didn't apply to them. They also made an extraordinary motion for a new trial on the basis of new evidence. (An extraordinary motion was the only way to get a Georgia court to consider voiding a previous conviction and granting a new trial.)

The new evidence was compelling. On February 20, the *Atlanta Journal* had published the news that Dr. Harris, who had performed Mary's autopsy, had known before the trial that the hair found on the lathe was not Mary's hair. He had told Dorsey, and the solicitor general had neither informed the defense of this evidence that would have cleared Leo nor allowed Dr. Harris to inform the court. Dorsey had simply gone ahead with his contention that Robert Barrett had found Mary Phagan's hair on the second floor, placing the scene of her murder near Leo's office, knowing that the evidence did not support this.

Henry Alexander, a former Georgia general assemblyman, joined the defense team. An established attorney who had prepared the documents to found the Atlanta Art Association (now the leading museum of art in the southeastern United States), Alexander brought an air of southern gentility to the defense. Although a member of Atlanta's Jewish community, Alexander was equally well respected by the city's Gentile population. In fact, at the University of Georgia, he had been Hugh Dorsey's roommate.

Alexander analyzed the letters found beside Mary's body for the defense. He pointed out that the old date on the order pad on which one letter was written suggested that the pad had originated in the basement, where old supplies were stored, not on the second floor,

Leo Frank's appeal attracted new allies to his case, including Jewish advertising magnate Albert Lasker (*left*). These allies helped Leo hire a new defense team, including Henry Alexander (*right*).

where current supplies were kept and where Jim Conley claimed Leo had dictated the letters to him.

More important, however, Alexander argued that the term "night witch" in the line "he said he wood love me land down play like the night witch did it" did not refer to "night watchman" as everyone had supposed. It actually referred to a specific haunt, or evil spirit, that many African American people believed in. The Baptist minister of Mary Phagan's own church confirmed this interpretation, saying he asked his black servant about "night witch" and she told him, "When the children cry out in their sleep at night, it means that the night witches are riding them, and if you don't go and wake them up, they will be found next morning strangled to death, with a cord around their necks." Alexander insisted that, given Leo's cultural background, there was no way Leo could have known this story to use the phrase in his dictation, as Dorsey had claimed.

Supporting Alexander's findings, Leo's lawyers discovered letters that Conley had written while he was in jail to a girl named Annie

Some Facts
about
The Murder Notes
in the
Phagan Case

_____

HENRY A. ALEXANDER

Above: Henry Alexander brought a measure of southern credibility to Frank's defense. The photo above shows him in college with prosecutor Hugh Dorsey. Years after the case, Alexander refused to attend a college reunion because Dorsey would be there—yet he kept this photo all his life.

Left and below: Alexander also took Frank's case to the public, distributing a pamphlet called *Some Facts about the Murder Notes in the Phagan Case.*

The First Note.

onal ench Co.

37 & 39 SOUTH FORSYTH ST.

ATLANTA, GA.   190

PUT THIS ORDER NUMBER ON YOUR BILL.

Bell Phone Main 171.   Order No. 1416

Written on yellow sheet. Found lying close to the head a few minutes after he arrived, by Police Sergeant L. S. Dobbs, at 3:25 A. M. Sunday morning, April 27, 1913, immediately after the discovery of the murder. The address "Mam" and the crowded condition of the page indicate that this was the note first written.
See its reading on next page.

Reading of note on opposite page with errors uncorrected:

"Mam   that negro hire down here did this   i went to make water and he push me down that hole   a long tall negro black   that hoo it wase   long sleam tall negro   i wright while play with me"

Reading with errors corrected:

"Mama: That negro hired down here did this.   I went to make water and he pushed me down that hole, a long tall negro, black, that who it was, long slim tall negro.   I write while play with me."*

*The purpose of the words "I write while play with me" was probably this: Realizing dimly that the question would arise how the girl mortally injured or dead could have done any writing, or how he, the murderer, standing over her and watching every movement, came to permit her to write notes incriminating himself, this was intended as an explanation. In other words, the reader of the notes was expected to believe that she wrote them without the murderer seeing her do it while he was "playing" with her.

5

4

Maud Carter. Their language and sentence structure matched the style of the letters found in the pencil factory, lending credence to the idea that Conley had not written them to anyone's dictation but had composed them himself. Alexander was so convinced that the evidence of the letters proved Leo's innocence and Conley's guilt, that he had his findings privately printed in pamphlet form. He distributed these pamphlets to the general population of Atlanta, hoping to turn popular opinion in Leo's favor.

The defense also had affidavits stating that many of Dorsey's witnesses had been coerced to lie or exaggerate, George Epps among them. The boy's testimony had already been refuted in court by the streetcar conductor. Later George said he had been encouraged to lie and continue lying, even after he admitted to Dorsey that his testimony was false.

A number of the girls who had been character witnesses against Leo stated that they had been told what to say, and one witness even swore he had overheard Conley telling another man that he had killed Mary himself. Annie Maud Carter signed an affidavit saying that Jim Conley had told her that he had beckoned to Mary in the pencil factory after she got her pay and then pushed her down the trapdoor into the basement and killed her. Even Helen Ferguson came forward with the new information that Jim Conley had tried to attack her in the factory the Saturday before Mary had been killed.

And a new witness, Mrs. J. B. Simmons, came forward with an affidavit that stated she had visited Atlanta on April 26. As she walked past the pencil factory at around 2:30, she heard a woman screaming for help from the basement. When she told the solicitor general, he tried to get her to say that she had actually heard the screams after 3:00, or at 1:30 instead of 2:30. "Mr. Dorsey wanted me to testify that it was at the time Mr. Frank was in the factory that I heard the screams, but I told him that I wasn't going to swear to an untruth just to help him or anyone else. I left him my address, expecting to be called as a witness at the trial, but that was the last I ever heard of it."

However, Dorsey argued against the extraordinary motion for a new trial, claiming that witnesses had been paid by the defense's investigators to give false statements. Some witnesses, like George Epps, did change their testimony back to the original version after being threatened by Dorsey. Others, like Mrs. Simmons, did not, and some of them paid for it. Minola McKnight was attacked at knifepoint, and slashed and beaten so badly that she refused to say anything about the case again.

On May 6, the court refused to grant the extraordinary motion. The defense appealed to the Georgia Supreme Court. In the twenty-first century, this type of appeal process would be drawn out. Prisoners on death row automatically have their cases appealed, and it may take many years before a convicted murderer sentenced to death is actually executed. But in 1914, few verdicts were appealed and executions were carried out a few months after the conviction. When lawyers did appeal a verdict, the courts did not take their time considering the case and giving a decision, as they do today. They ruled quickly and decisively.

Leo barely had time to get his hopes up before the Georgia Supreme Court ruled, on June 6, to deny the defense motion to set aside the conviction on the grounds of failure to allow the defendant due process. When his attorneys took the motion to the Fulton County Superior Court, he hoped for success again, only to have the Superior Court deny the motion as well.

But Leo continued to hope. His attorneys appealed that ruling to the Georgia Supreme Court and also continued arguing the extraordinary motion for a new trial based on new evidence. But on October 14, the Georgia Supreme Court upheld the lower court's denial of the extraordinary motion for a new trial, discounting the new evidence. And on November 17, the same court ruled against setting aside the original guilty verdict.

A new execution date was set for January 22, 1915. But Leo and his supporters refused to give up. Albert Lasker wrote to Leo that he was very glad to see "that the same courageous spirit which has always been with you during your terrible martyrdom is still buoying you up. . . . The courage that your own consciousness of innocence gives you is helping you bridge over the awful chasm of this persecution."

Leo's attorneys took the case all the way to the U.S. Supreme Court, asking the justices to issue a legal document, or writ, of *habeas corpus*. In Latin, *habeas corpus* means "You shall have the body." Under U.S. law, prisoners can petition for such a writ to obtain their freedom when they believe they are being held unlawfully. The defense team argued that Leo was being held in prison illegally since he had been denied due process by not being allowed in court when he was sentenced.

Louis Marshall of the American Jewish Committee traveled to Washington, D.C., to present this argument himself, writing that "I was not in the case as paid counsel, but that I had embarked upon it, because I felt that I owed a duty to the profession, to the cause of justice." The Supreme Court agreed to hear the case.

While the defense presented evidence of the crowd's shouts and threats, Solicitor General Dorsey argued, "We showed by witnesses that none of the alleged demonstrations in the court room during Frank's trial and none of those alleged to have occurred in the streets outside the court house ever came to the attention of the jury."

On April 9, 1915, after Leo had been in jail for nearly two years, the Supreme Court rejected this last appeal, 7–2. The majority decision stated that Leo's attorneys had waived the right to argue that the accused had been denied due process because they had not raised the objection in a timely manner.

Not all the justices agreed. Oliver Wendell Holmes and Charles Evans Hughes dissented, arguing that "Mob law does not become due process of law by securing the assent of a terrorized jury." But their distress didn't help Leo Frank. His execution was now set for June 22, 1915, and his only hopes were to petition the Georgia Prison Commission and then the governor of Georgia, for clemency to mercifully sentence him to life in prison instead of death. Stunned, Leo told reporters, "It is so hideous, but at the same time, so unreal, so incongruous."

On May 31, 1915, the defense appealed to the Georgia Prison Commission for clemency. The defense was denied by a 2–1 vote on June 9. The dissenting commissioner, Thomas Patterson, believed that it would be unforgivable to send a man to death on the testimony of an accomplice, when that accomplice appeared to be the guilty man. But he was unable to convince the other two commissioners.

Leo could not understand why his appeals had been ruled against on every turn. The evidence that he had not gotten a fair trial seemed overwhelming. As he had asked throughout the appeals process, "Can it be that the law, and our system of its administration, is so inexorable that truth and innocence may never be heard after once the die is cast? Is the door forever closed and the way barred?"

Supreme Court justice Oliver Wendell Holmes. The justice was one of two members of the Supreme Court of the United States who dissented in the court's decision not to overturn Frank's conviction.

"JEW MONEY HAS DEBASED US"

THE COURT OF PUBLIC OPINION

Why did every court rule against Leo Frank? For a start, each court's decision had to be based on points of law, not common sense. An appeals court could only decide whether the law had been followed in the original trial and whether the attorneys had followed the law governing appeals after the original trial was over. None of the judges could retry the case to reach a decision. They could only rule on the information the defense attorneys were allowed to give them in their legal briefs. Well might Leo ask, "Is the technical finesse of the law to forever preclude a hearing of facts, and human right to be trampled beneath the judicial feet?" Indeed, the courts could not apply the common sense that was beginning to be expressed across the entire United States.

Collier's Weekly published a detailed exposé about the case, and newspaper editorials (even in papers published in every southern state) expressed horror that any citizen could be tried by innuendo and prejudice. They begged for some court, any court, to overturn the conviction and give Leo Frank the opportunity for a fair trial. Citizens spoke out in protest, even in Atlanta, where Dr. A. R. Holderby, pastor of the First Christian Church, stated, "If the evidence against this unfortunate man is true—if there is no reasonable doubt—then he ought to suffer the penalty. But it would be unfair to hang a sheep killing dog upon the evidence upon which Frank has been convicted."

In December 1914, after the Georgia Supreme Court denied the second appeal, the defense asked Judge Roan if he would recommend that the governor grant Leo clemency. Judge Roan wrote, "It is possible that I showed undue deference to the opinion of the jury in this case, when I allowed their verdict to stand. They said by their verdict that they had found the truth. I was still in a state of uncertainty, and so expressed myself. . . .

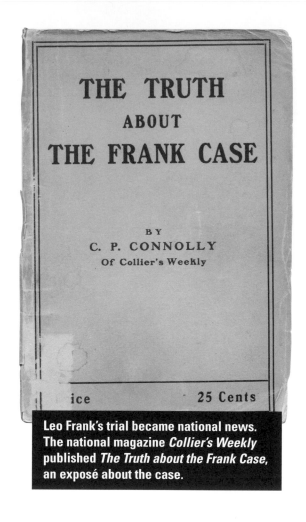

THE TRUTH
ABOUT
THE FRANK CASE

BY
C. P. CONNOLLY
Of Collier's Weekly

ice   25 Cents

Leo Frank's trial became national news. The national magazine *Collier's Weekly* published *The Truth about the Frank Case,* an exposé about the case.

I allowed the jury's verdict to remain undisturbed. I had no way of knowing it was erroneous." Roan did say that he would urge the governor to consider the case "at the proper time," but would not agree to do so immediately, even though he knew he was in failing health and near death. He concluded with, "If by any cause I am prevented from doing this, you are at liberty to use this letter at the hearing."

In fact, Roan was so unsure about how he had handled the trial that he admitted his doubts to J. J. Barge, an Atlanta attorney. Barge told the judge that if he had felt the same uncertainty that Roan expressed, Barge would "certainly have granted a new trial. [Roan] then said, 'Well, suppose I had, then that dreadful mob spirit would have broken out again, and now when it goes to the Supreme Court and comes back, maybe he can get a fair trial.'"

Powerful figures in southern politics like Tom Watson (*above*) used the Frank trial to generate support for their own causes.

That mob spirit came from more than prejudice against Leo because he was a northern industrialist. It came from more than sexual prejudice against a man accused of violating a southern woman. It also came from religious prejudice against Leo because he was Jewish. That he was a Yankee Jew only made things worse.

The mob spirit and religious prejudice were fed by one particular politician named Tom Watson. Watson had served in the U.S. House of Representatives, had run as the vice-presidential candidate on the Populist Party ticket with William Jennings Bryan in 1896, and had run for president himself in 1904. In 1913 he still exerted considerable power over Georgia's Democratic Party and, through his magazines, over Georgia's voters. Watson took the sparks of anti-Semitism and fanned them into a fire that threatened to devastate Atlanta as absolutely as Sherman's fires had in the War Between the States.

Despite that most Atlanta citizens thought well of their Jewish community in general, they were quick to follow Watson's lead. In stirring up public opinion against Leo Frank, reporters and public speakers were willing to use the word "Jew" as if it were an even stronger curse than "murderer." Tom Watson, who claimed he spoke for the Gentile, or non-Jewish, poor and rural people of Georgia, aggressively encouraged this attitude.

Watson asked "Does a Jew expect extraordinary favors and immunities *because* of his race?" and denounced Leo as a wealthy Jew who thought his money gave him the right to prey upon poor southern girls. That was quite a different picture of Leo from the relatively poor man his friends knew. Louis White Fehr had been a classmate of Leo's at Cornell, a school with many wealthy students, and wrote during the trial that "when I knew Mr. Frank in college he was a young man who lived modestly without a large allowance."

But no one who read Tom Watson's magazine wanted to know what a New Yorker thought about Leo Frank. These readers already resented Leo because they believed that wealthy northern Jews were paying for his legal battle. Watson screamed, "Jew money has debased us, bought us, and sold us—and laughs at us." He sneered at Leo's supporters (mostly Jewish), who were trying to raise money for his appeals, writing,

> The [Jewish] Finance Committee and its cooperative
> organizations do not intend that Frank shall be punished
> at all, for the rape and murder he committed on the
> Gentile girl.
> In their eyes she was legitimate prey; and with their
> Unlimited Money and Invisible Power, they have
> established the precedent in Georgia that no Jew shall
> suffer capital punishment for a crime committed on a
> Gentile.
> In the name of God, what are the people to do?

Watson stirred up religious prejudice against Jews to the point that some Christian citizens of Atlanta were moved to threaten anyone who supported Leo. While Leo's lawyers worked on his appeal, they were bombarded by anonymous telephone calls threatening, "If they don't hang that Jew, we'll hang you."

This fury against Jews got to the point that people who privately sympathized with Leo feared violent retribution. One Kansas reporter, sent to observe the appeal process, wrote:

> The managing editor, associate editor, city editor,
> assistant city editor and court reporter of an Atlanta
> newspaper said to me they knew Frank was entitled to a
> new trial; his trial was not fair.

"Then why don't you say so?" I asked.

"We dare not; we would be accused of being bought by Jew money," they answered.

What judge would be willing to reverse Leo's original conviction on the basis of facts if it meant facing such accusations, especially when he could base his ruling on legal technicalities and spare himself the charge of being bought by Jews?

Only one person in authority proved willing and able to ignore emotion and prejudice, and take a clear-eyed new look at Leo Frank's conviction.

"RESPONSIBILITY RESTS WHERE THE POWER IS REPOSED"

THE GOVERNOR'S CONSCIENCE

Governor John Slaton had hoped to leave office unscathed by the emotional turmoil of Mary Phagan's murder and Leo Frank's trial. He had his own political ambitions and intended to use the governor's seat as a stepping-stone on the way to the U.S. Senate. Tom Watson and other Georgia statesmen had promised their support for his campaign, and he was eager to get started. His gubernatorial successor, Nat Harris, was due to take office on June 26, 1915, and Slaton assumed that if Leo Frank's petition for clemency came to the governor's office, Harris would be the one who would have to deal with it.

But Leo's petition came to Slaton before he left office, and no sooner had he received it than he began to receive warnings. Watson

John M. Slaton was the governor of Georgia from 1911 to 1912 and 1913 to 1915.

let Slaton know that if the governor would deny clemency and let Leo hang, Watson would use his power to get Slaton elected U.S. senator and would make him the dominant force in Georgia politics for the next twenty years. If Slaton granted clemency, Watson would give his considerable support to someone else.

Threatening Governor Slaton was not a wise move. John Slaton was an unusual politician: a man with a conscience. Watson's "offer," probably beyond any other consideration, prompted him to examine the Leo Frank case closely. He had already gone on record the previous year as believing, "If Leo M. Frank is guilty, he ought to be hanged. If he is not guilty, then he ought to be saved." And the governor seemed unmoved by the prejudice that had swept much of his constituency. He said, "Frank shall not be a victim of injustice because he is a Jew. I don't want the impression to go out that the governor of Georgia could not give justice to a Jew."

On the morning of June 12, 1915, Governor Slaton reluctantly opened hearings on Leo's petition for clemency. Leo's lawyers weren't asking the governor to grant a pardon and say that Leo should not be punished at all for Mary's murder. They were asking him to commute Leo's death sentence to life imprisonment. This was partly due to Leo's insistence that asking for a pardon would be as much as confessing guilt. He didn't want to be pardoned for a crime he had not committed—he wanted justice. His lawyers were also worried about the angry mood in Atlanta. They had good reason to be concerned.

When the prison commission had heard their petition only two weeks earlier, nearly one thousand people had gathered in Marietta, Mary's hometown, in a meeting to protest granting clemency. The meeting started with the cry, "Let him hang!" and built to its climax with the angry announcement: "Mary Phagan was a poor factory girl. What show would she have against Jew money? When they found they couldn't fool the people of Georgia, they got people from Massachusetts, New York and California to try and raise trouble. Well, we throw the advice of these outsiders back in their teeth."

The group sent a delegation to inform the commission of the depth of their feelings. Leo's lawyers suspected that Atlanta would explode in riots and Leo might be attacked before he could be taken out of the city if they asked for a pardon and received it. So they petitioned the governor for commutation of Leo's death sentence to life in prison.

Governor Slaton conducted intensive hearings. He visited the factory and explored the office area, the metal shop, and the basement. He read through the transcripts, legal briefs, and all documents relating to the case. And he considered the affidavits of Will Green, William Mincey, and others who had sworn they heard Jim Conley confess to the murder.

The governor also considered the letter Judge Roan had written before his death, saying that he would urge the governor to consider clemency. He considered a letter sent him by Colonel P. H. Brewster, who had been one of Hugh Dorsey's law partners at the time of Leo's original trial. Brewster said that based on the facts he learned at the law office, he was certain that Leo Frank was innocent. He even urged the governor to publish his letter so that the public would know the truth.

Slaton spoke with people outside of the hearings. Deputy Clerk of the Court Frank Myers told the governor that Judge Roan had told him in the men's room that the solicitor general who had preceded Hugh Dorsey would have asked the jury to find Leo not guilty. One of the jailers, Mr. Tuggle, told the governor that "if he had been left for a few days longer in charge of the prisoners, he was convinced from the way Jim Conley talked, that Conley would have admitted committing the offense, but the Chief of Detectives said that he didn't care anything about convicting a negro for the murder. That, of course, was the usual course of events, but it would be a feather in his cap if he could convict a white man and a Jew."

John Boykin, who would later be elected solicitor general, wrote to Slaton that he had spoken with William Smith, Jim Conley's lawyer, and Smith had told him that Conley had admitted to committing the murder. Smith felt, however, that he could not disclose this admission publicly because of attorney-client privilege, which protects the privacy of conversations between lawyers and those they represent. But he had issued a statement that "Leo M. Frank is innocent, and that if a proper cooperation of officials can be secured I have absolute faith that the mystery of the death of Mary Phagan will be solved to the satisfaction of every reasonable man in the community."

The governor himself spoke at length with Smith. The lawyer would not confirm that Conley had confessed to him, but he pointed out that police had never matched the bloody handprints in the basement to Leo Frank. In 1913 people who were arrested were not automatically fingerprinted, so Jim Conley had never been printed. Smith had attempted several times to take the man's fingerprints to compare them with the prints on the basement door, but Conley always resisted.

Smith had not been in court while Conley testified, at Dorsey's request. When he later read Conley's trial testimony, Smith was stunned. Having spoken to his client a good deal, Smith saw that the man who read newspapers avidly (especially the ones with articles about him) and who discussed the news and the trial with his attorney had disguised his true intelligence on the stand to win over the jury. He presented himself as the simple black man that the white jury would most expect to see and would most easily believe. In jail Conley often spoke articulately, yet on the stand, he had used simple words and a more familiar black dialect.

In addition to listening to Smith, considering correspondence with other attorneys, interviewing people involved in the proceedings, and examining the case in detail, Governor Slaton also read his mail. He received over one hundred thousand letters from citizens and statesmen all over the United States requesting clemency. Even children like Marjorie Smith, of Loudonville, Ohio, had written:

> *I heard of Leo Frank in the press.*
> *He does not look guilty there.*
> *I am only ten years old, but I know something about*
> *the ways of men, how they treat their wives when they are*
> *drunk.*

I am not old as you know, but for my sake release Leo Frank.

Yours, truly,
Marjorie Smith

P.S. Write soon.

The world outside of Georgia seemed solidly in support of Leo Frank. But Slaton also received numerous letters from Georgians demanding that he let the sentence of the court stand. The governor considered both evidence and public opinion before making up his mind.

Saturday afternoon, June 19, 1915, Slaton sat down to write a twenty-nine-page document explaining his findings. He carefully laid out the facts of the case, both those that seemed to incriminate Leo and those that appeared to exonerate him. And he described his own careful research at the pencil factory. The governor ended by saying that there was considerable new evidence that had never been introduced at trial, such as Dr. Harris's admission that the hairs on the lathe were not Mary's. Legally, there were strong grounds for commuting Leo's death sentence.

Governor Slaton finished his document on Sunday but delayed announcing his decision. Around 11:30 that night, he sent the sheriff orders to transfer Leo to the Georgia State Prison Farm at Milledgeville on the 12:01 train to Macon. The sheriff awakened Leo and rushed him to the train station. At Macon they hired a local taxi cab company to drive them to the prison farm. A group of about ten men surrounded the car, and one told Leo, referring to another Georgia town along the railroad route, "You're lucky to save your neck. You are lucky you came through Griffin without anyone knowing that you were on the train." Throughout the drive, Leo seemed to have difficulty believing that he was actually being reprieved from execution. He was convinced that cars were following him and he'd never reach the prison farm safely.

The news broke on Monday morning: Governor Slaton had commuted Leo's sentence. He explained his decision by writing, "The performance of my duty under the Constitution is a matter of conscience. The responsibility rests where the power is reposed. . . . I can endure misconstruction, abuse and condemnation, but I cannot stand the constant companionship of an accusing conscience, which would remind me in every thought that I, as governor of Georgia, failed to do what I thought to be right."

Georgia erupted in fury. Although newspaper editors and politicians outside of the state would praise his courageous decision, Hugh Dorsey denounced Governor Slaton and Tom Watson railed against him in print, "Our grand old Empire State HAS BEEN RAPED!" A mob of four thousand angry people armed with guns and bricks and shouting, "Pay the Governor a call!" marched toward the governor's mansion, where Slaton waited with his wife and a dozen friends who were armed with rifles or pistols, prepared to defend the governor. Chief Beavers met the mob with fifty mounted officers but stopped only about half of the people. The state militia was called out. When the mob arrived at the mansion, they attacked the militia with rocks and broken bottles, but the soldiers were able to force them back.

Then word arrived that two hundred people from Marietta were on their way. This mob had already hanged Slaton in effigy over a sign, "John M. Slaton, King of the Jews and Traitor Governor of Georgia." Then they burned the mannequin and headed for Atlanta. When the mob saw the militia, however, they stopped short.

In Newnan another mob hanged effigies of both Slaton and Frank, set them on fire, and dragged them through the streets. And in Columbus, a mob hanged Slaton in effigy and then used the figure for target practice. Rumors flew that a group of 150 people in Marietta had met at Mary Phagan's grave. They called themselves the Knights of Mary Phagan, and swore to punish both Governor Slaton and Leo Frank, no matter how long they had to wait.

The Marietta Vigilance Committee passed out flyers to Jewish storeowners warning them, "You are hereby notified to close up this business and quit Marietta by Saturday night, June 26, 1915 or else stand the consequences. We mean to rid Marietta of all Jews by the above date. You can heed this warning or stand the punishment the committee may see fit to deal out to you."

Governor Slaton was widely attacked for his decision in the Frank case. The sign beneath his hanging effigy reads, "John M. Slaton the King of Jews."

Atlanta Jewish merchants organized groups to keep watch over their shops, attempting to protect them from angry rioters. At the same time, they kept their children indoors, afraid they might be attacked. Jewish families in Marietta also stayed out of sight, hoping the violence would blow over. In Atlanta the mob stormed the governor's mansion a second time and martial law was briefly declared.

On June 26, during the inauguration ceremonies for Slaton's successor, Nat Harris, a man attacked Slaton with a thick iron pipe. Major Polhill Wheeler of the National Guard pulled the man away. Shaken, Slaton still managed to speak out at the luncheon honoring the new governor. He told the people of Atlanta,

> *Honest people may disagree with me, an honest man, but we realize that we must be measured by our consciences. Two thousand years ago another Governor [Pontius Pilate] washed his hands of a case and turned a Jew [Jesus] over to a mob. For two thousand years that Governor's name has been accursed. If today another Jew were lying in his grave because I had failed to do my duty I would all through life find his blood on my hands and would consider myself an assassin through cowardice.*

Once the new governor was in office, John Slaton and his wife left Georgia. Several weeks afterward, Mayor James Woodward of Atlanta said, "I have been friends with [Jack Slaton], and while I hate to say it, I would not advise him to return to Georgia for a year—if ever." Saddened by the way his constituents had turned on him, Slaton did not return to Georgia for many years, and when he finally returned, he never again served in public office.

Hugh Dorsey, vigorously supported by Tom Watson (who was himself elected U.S. senator), would be elected governor of Georgia in 1917 by a landslide.

"I AM ALIVE BY A BIG MAJORITY"

ATTACK

Leo arrived at the Georgia State Prison Farm at Milledgeville feeling ill, and wrote Lucille immediately to assure her he was getting better:

> *My dear Honey:*
>
> *I received several letters today & several wires. I expect that you are a trifle "under the weather" over the storm through which we have passed. It has indeed been an ordeal for both of us my darling but in time both of us will be happy. My health is improving though my cold is still with me. My appetite too is improving. After that which I have gone through, it will take some time before I gain my poise & physical balance. I will let you & my parents know just when it will be best for you to come to see me for the first time. . . .*
>
> *With much love to all & a large share for you, I am*
> *Your loving husband*
> *Leo*

Once his health improved, Leo was issued the striped prison uniform that identified him as the lowest grade prisoner and became known simply as Convict No. 965. He quickly settled into a routine that was almost a relief after his long months in the tower. Working and exercising regularly was a definite improvement after his confinement. Friends and family sent him food and supplies, from stationery and stamps to a gramophone and audio recordings, and his parents wrote him often. Nearly every envelope contained a letter about the case from his father, an affectionate letter from his mother about friends and family, and a much scrawled and blotted note from his niece, Eleanore, usually along the lines of:

> *Dear uncle Leo and aunt Lucille,*
> *I send you many kisses from me & brother Robert.*
>
> > *Your niece,*
> > *Eleanore*

After he finished his prison chores, Leo would write letters. He wrote to friends and to acquaintances who supported his appeals, assuring them that the commutation would give him the opportunity to pursue his quest for justice. Leo was particularly touched by the youngsters who wrote to him. Soon after his arrival in Milledgeville, he received a telegram from Jesse Berkovitz of Tuscaloosa, Alabama:

> *I congratulate you and the governor of Georgia. I hope*
> *the truth will be found out and you will some day be*
> *free. I am 11 years old and have read the papers and*
> *can't believe you guilty.*

Leo wrote back to Jesse on July 6:

> *My dear little friend,*
> *Allow me to thank you for your telegram of June 21. I*
> *was profoundly touched by your tender thought of me.*
> *It surely can not be long before I am free and vindicated,*
> *and right and innocence come into their own.*

With the assurance of my every good wish, I am,
cordially yours,
Leo M. Frank

Leo believed what he wrote to Jesse. He
confidently expected to win a new trial and be
exonerated in the future. He anticipated returning to
work and wrote often to Herbert Schiff, who was now
acting as superintendent at the pencil factory, asking
about production and questioning activities such as
taking inventory.

Leo treasured Lucille's frequent visits, even though
they could see each other only in the presence of a
guard. When she wasn't visiting, he wrote her daily.

> *My own:*
> *I trust that you arrived home safely after a*
> *pleasant trip. I did so much enjoy having you*
> *with me. Your presence was a tonic and an*
> *inspiration. I look forward to your next visit here*
> *to me.*

But in less than a month, Leo's routine in the
prison farm would be interrupted, not by the news
that he had won a new trial but by an unexpected
attack on the night of July 17, 1915. While Leo slept, another
prisoner, J. William Creen, slashed Leo's throat with a butcher's
knife—something no prisoner should have been able to obtain.

Leo nearly bled to death before two other prisoners who
happened to be doctors were able to stitch the severed jugular vein
and close the wound. Dr. G. D. Compton, the prison doctor, arrived
about fifteen minutes later, but that would have been too late without
the quick action of the other men.

When he recovered enough to speak, Leo told the doctor, "If I
am going to die, I am not afraid. Nothing stands between me and
God. I hope that the man who attacked me will be forgiven." As if to

Leo Frank recovered from his first attack in this prison hospital ward in the summer of 1915.

himself, he whispered, "I guess they have got me now."

Lucille was called around 1 A.M. and rushed to her husband's side. She wrote, "He's so weak, but so brave. He looks at me and smiles such a dear smile. When I came into the room he could barely make himself understood but he whispered 'Angel.'" She sat by his side all night, holding his hand and fanning him.

Tom Watson lost no time in celebrating the attack and viciously taunted Leo in his magazine by claiming, "The butcher-knife used had been in operation during the day *killing hogs*." This idea that a knife used for hog killing might be used to cut a Jew's throat was a cruel mockery of the Jewish dietary prohibition against eating pork.

CIRCULATION
Yesterday, Sat.
47,944

THE ATLANTA CONSTITUTION

CIRCULATION
LAST SUNDAY.
49,847

Vol. XLVIII—No. 33.   ATLANTA, GA., SUNDAY MORNING, JULY 18, 1915.—FORTY-EIGHT PAGES.   Daily and Sunday, carrier delivery, 12 cents weekly.
Single copies on the streets and at news stands 5 cents

LEO FRANK'S THROAT CUT BY STATE FARM PRISONER

Grave Element Is Added By Attack on the Orduna To the Strained Relations Of America and Germany

Should the First Reports Be Confirmed by Official Investigation the Incident Will Greatly Influence the President and Cabinet in Formulating Next Step Regarding the Activities of German Submarines.

THEORY THAT GERMANY HAD CHANGED METHODS DISSIPATED BY ATTACK

Washington Is Shocked by Attack on Vessel After Information From Berlin That the Submarine Commanders Had Been Warned to Exercise Great Care. Incident Increases Uneasiness Felt Since Last German Note Failed to Give Assurances Asked by the United States.

Washington, July 17.—Into the grave situation that has developed between the United States and Germany over the sinking of the Lusitania was thrust another issue today, when it was revealed that the British steamer Orduna, carrying a score of Americans, had been attacked by a German submarine.

Should first reports of an attempt to torpedo without warning be borne out by the official investigation about to be instigated, it was indicated in official quarters that the thrust there probably would regard the incident as adding a grave element to the already strained relations between the two countries.

Lacking information as to the circumstances of the attack, officials were unable to predict tonight to what extent the Orduna case would aggravate the situation, but they thought the question would certainly compel serious consideration by President Wilson and his cabinet in formulating the next step in the policy of the United States toward the activities of German submarines and the safety of Americans on the high seas.

GERMAN PRACTICES REMAIN THE SAME.

Although the Orduna escaped unhurt, this, in view of officials, does not relieve the case of grave possibilities. The fact that a belligerent merchant ship bound for the United States with Americans on board and without arms and ammunition or contraband

Continued on Page Five.

The Season of Change

People shake themselves out of fixed habits in the summer months. They move about more.

They devote less time to work and more to recreation.

It seems natural that they should be particularly open to changes in their buying routine and that warm weather would be a good time to advertise.

To the strangers passing through the city your mes-

BY HALF SECOND ORDUNA ESCAPED LUSITANIA'S FATE

Torpedo Fired by German Submarine Churned the Water Ten Feet Behind the Liner's Rudder.

PASSENGERS SLEEPING WHEN ATTACK WAS MADE

Twenty-Two Americans on the Ship—Baroness Rosenkrantz, Formerly Miss Rebie Lowe, of Atlanta, on Board With Her Husband. Thrilling Story of Liner's Escape.

New York, July 17.—The Cunard liner Orduna, from Liverpool to New York, with 227 passengers, including twenty-two Americans, was attacked without warning, it was learned on her arrival here today, by a German submarine on the morning of July 9.

Twenty miles from the graveyard of the Lusitania, off Old Head of Kinsale, the Orduna escaped the Lusitania's fate by one-half second of time or ten feet of space. The German torpedo churning the water that distance behind the liner's rudder. Then the Orduna sped away, she was followed by the submarine, which rose to the surface, manned a gun and shelled the fleeing steamer.

PASSENGERS MOSTLY ASLEEP.

The attack was timed at 1:50 o'clock by the morning, when all but a few of her passengers were asleep. Aroused by stewards, the passengers dressed hurriedly and went to the upper deck, where they donned life belts and took their places at the lifeboats. They heard the scream of the shells and saw the ocean spit up columns of water where the missiles struck. When the fire grew hot, they were ordered, for their own protection, to the next deck below.

They had not seen the Orduna showed her heels to the assailant. Through marine glasses the passengers watched the low-lying German warship coming up with a boat in her teeth, but the Orduna's flight was faster than the pursuit, and after several shots had been fired, without effect, the submarine gave up the chase.

A wireless call for help was sent out by the Orduna when the torpedo was seen. She was then 31 miles south of Queenstown. The reply, Captain Taylor says in his official report, was that help would be given within an hour. It was four hours before the first British vessel, a small armored yacht, the Deninette, appeared.

AMERICAN OFFICIAL TO MAKE PROTEST.

Protest will be made to the American government by at least one citizen of the United States, and possibly others, who were aboard. William G. Thompson, of Chicago, counsel to the federal industrial relations commission, who went abroad in his official capacity with that March, and was returning to make his report, is the passenger who said today that he would make vigorous protest to his government.

"As an American citizen, employed in an official capacity by the government to go abroad, I feel that I should bring the government's attention to the attack," said Mr. Thompson. "I felt that I had a right to return home on the Orduna, although she flies the British flag, because she is

Continued on Page Ten.

Free Tea To

Desperately Wounded by Fellow-Prisoner

LEO M. FRANK

DRIVE OF TEUTONS AGAINST RUSSIANS GATHERING FORCE

Vast Movement Is Begun by Germany and Austria Which Has for Object the Encircling of the Czar's Armies.

FIGHTING ALSO HEAVY ON THE WESTERN FRONT

At Various Points Germans Have Furiously Attacked the French Lines, but Paris Claims All Attacks Have Been Repulsed.

London, July 17.—Continuation of the heavy fighting of the past few days which has tossed the lines of one side to and fro along the battle front in France is indicated in the

---

"At Peace With God, Ready To Die," Says Leo M. Frank, Wants Assailant Pardoned

Milledgeville, Ga., July 17.—After Frank's wound had been dressed, he turned to the physicians attending him

If Frank survives the attack it will be because of the prompt attention given him by Dr. McNaughton, it was

---

Jugular Vein Severed Partially, Has Slight Chance For Recovery

Attacked by William Creen, Convicted Murderer, at 11:10 Last Night, Frank's Condition Is Critical, According to Prison Officials. Was Asleep in Prison Dormitory When Creen Rushed Upon Him—Physicians Sew Up the Wound and Operation May Save Life.

"SEEMS THAT THEY HAVE GOT ME,"
HE MUTTERED WHEN DISCOVERED
BLEEDING ON FLOOR BY GUARDS

Creen Made Attack With Butcher Knife Smuggled Into Prison—Rushed Upon Him in Dark. Frank, Though Weak and Sinking Slowly, Retains Consciousness and Directs Physicians How to Stop Flow of Blood—Creen Confesses, and Says He Is Sorry.

Milledgeville, Ga., July 18.—At 3 o'clock this morning Dr. Compton, the prison surgeon, stated that Frank's chances for recovery are slight.

"There is danger of blood poisoning," said the doctor. "There is danger of the stitches in the jugular vein slipping, either one of which might cause death."

Milledgeville, Ga., July 17.—Leo M. Frank, serving a life imprisonment sentence for the murder of Mary Phagan, a 14-year-old Atlanta factory girl, was attacked and his throat cut by William Creen, a fellow prisoner, at the state prison farm here. Physicians announced late tonight that the wounded man's condition was serious, but that he had a chance to recover.

The attack on Frank was made while he was sleeping in the prison dormitory in company with the other inmates. The knife used was made of a file and had been used by the prisoners in killing hogs during the day. Frank's throat was cut for a distance of several inches and the jugular vein partially severed.

Some animosity has been shown Frank since he arrived at the state prison farm after his death sentence was commuted to life imprisonment, but the prison officials said tonight that they had not thought for an instant that an attack would be made on him.

William Creen, 45 years old, who is doing a life term from Columbus, Ga., on a charge of murder, has confessed to cutting Frank's throat. Creen has been put in a dungeon.

Doctors completed sewing up the wound in Frank's throat at 1:15 o'clock this morning. The knife had joined the jugular vein, and they believed the operation was successful. Frank was taken to the hospital. He was still conscious.

The inmates of the prison occupy one large room at night, a sort of dormitory, where the strictest of rules are observed by the prisoners. All are allowed the freedom of the floor until 8 o'clock, but after that hour a prisoner is not allowed to move without permission from a guard.

The attack on Frank tonight came so quick that no guard had time to interfere. Creen is alleged to have
here he had

Creen, however, told authorities that he had slipped the knife from the kitchen and hidden it in his cot. At first he said he had been called from "one on high" to kill Leo but later said, "I felt that as long as he was here there was danger of the prison being attacked. I was afraid the guards and the people making the attack would shoot at each other and people would be killed, so I came to the conclusion that it was my duty to save the people from the danger to which Frank's presence exposed them."

Several days later, Leo asked Dr. Compton if he thought he would live. When the doctor assured him that he would, Leo said, "I am going to live. I must live. I must vindicate myself."

His courage and determination inspired the friends who had supported him all along. Herbert Haas wrote to Lucille that Leo's "every action is but a credit to his friends, and that I am proud to know a man with the character and stamina of Leo."

At first Lucille hired nurses to be with him around the clock. As he improved, she took over the nursing job. Leo's humor returned along with the confidence that he would soon have the opportunity to continue seeking justice. He wrote to his mother:

> Just a few words to let you know that I am improving
> daily & that my dear Lucille is well & on the job. We let
> the night nurse go & the day nurse will take her place,
> dear Lucille holding the fort in the daytime.
>   I hope you did not yesterday or today hear the rumor I
> heard—viz [namely]: that I was dead. I want to firmly
> and decisively deny that rumor. I am alive by a big
> majority.

"CALMNESS AND DIGNITY"

DEATH SENTENCE

Shortly after John Slaton left Georgia, several men in authority got together in Marietta to discuss what they should do about the commutation of Leo Frank's sentence. These were not rough, uneducated countrymen but men who represented Georgia's finest families and greatest statesmen: a former governor, a former mayor, and several active political figures.

These powerful men made their plans and then looked for other men to carry them out. They selected a merchant, a lawyer, and the man who ran the county convict camp to be in charge. The group began looking for others to assist them. This was fairly straightforward. A man would simply approach a person he'd like to draft (many of them Knights of Mary Phagan) and ask him if he wanted to participate. If he declined, there were no hard feelings. If he accepted, he was one of them.

The group wanted to keep things orderly, so they were looking for certain types of men. They especially wanted anyone with law enforcement experience and individuals with particular skills. For example, one man owned a garage that could get cars in shape, while another was an electrician. Eventually, the group came to include sheriffs, deputies, police officers, two bankers, Mary Phagan's uncle, and the mayor of Marietta.

One of the planners described the participants as men "whose worth was known collectively and individually, who were resolved to bear any burden and go through with their plans at any cost." Their scheme was to contact officials at the Georgia State Prison Farm at

Milledgeville in advance so they would be able to enter and leave without doing any damage, remove the prisoner with dignity but with firmness, and take Leo Frank to Marietta in Cobb County where they would finally carry out the sentence of the jury.

On August 16, 1915, seven automobiles left Marietta carrying this group of men. They left at different times, so nobody would notice them, and then met up with one another. The cars reached the prison farm around 9 P.M. where "Yellow Jacket" Brown, the electrician, was waiting for them. He promptly cut nearly all the town's phone lines.

At the prison, an inmate heard the cars on the prison farm road. Aware that threats had been made against their famous prisoner, he asked the guards to send Leo to safety. But one of the prison officials who had been contacted in advance told the man it was probably just joyriders.

THE LYNCH PARTY

Not all of the men involved in the planning and lynching of Leo Frank have yet been identified, but those whose names are known are:

GOVERNMENT OFFICIALS AND EMPLOYEES

JOSEPH M. BROWN, former governor of Georgia

EMMET BURTON, police officer

EUGENE HERBERT CLAY, former mayor of Marietta

E. P. DOBBS, current mayor of Marietta

WILLIAM J. FREY, former Cobb County sheriff

GEORGE HICKS, Cobb County deputy sheriff

WILLIAM MCKINNEY, Cobb County deputy sheriff

NEWTON AUGUSTUS MORRIS, superior court judge

NEWTON MAYES MORRIS, in charge of the Cobb County chain gang

FRED MORRIS, Georgia general assemblyman

GEORGE SWANSON, Cobb County sheriff

OTHER PARTICIPANTS

JOHN AUGUSTUS BENSON, merchant

D. R. BENTON, Mary Phagan's uncle

"YELLOW JACKET" BROWN, electrician

BOLAN GLOVER BRUMBY, manufacturer

JIM BRUMBY, garage owner, serviced the cars

LUTHER BURTON, coal yard operator

GEORGE EXIE DANIELL, merchant

CICERO HOLTON DOBBS, taxi driver

JOHN TUCKER DORSEY, lawyer

C. D. ELDER, physician

GORDON BAXTER GANN, lawyer

ROBERT A. HILL, banker, helped fund the operation

HORACE HAMBY, farmer

LAWRENCE HANEY, farmer

RALPH MOLDEN MANNING, contractor

L. B. ROBESON, railroad freight agent, provided a car

MOULTRIE MCKINNEY SESSIONS, lawyer and banker

"COON" SHAW, mule trader

The men from Marietta had a map of the farm and wasted no time in seizing and disarming the warden and the superintendent, finding Leo, and hauling him out of bed. Leo asked permission to dress, but someone in the group told him he wouldn't need clothes where he was going. They handcuffed him and dragged him in only his nightshirt to one of the waiting cars. Then one of the men told the prison staff that they were taking Leo to Marietta, where they would hang him over Mary Phagan's grave, and the caravan drove away.

When the warden tried to call for assistance, he discovered the phone lines had been cut. It took several hours to find an undamaged phone line and place a call to Atlanta. By the time the police had been notified, it was too late to stop the lynch party.

While they drove to Marietta, several of the men in the car that carried Leo tried to get him to confess. One asked him if he had killed the Phagan girl, but he said nothing. Another man asked, "Is there anything you would like to say before your execution?"

Leo said, "No," his voice so low they could barely hear it over the engine.

As they drove through Alpharetta, about twenty miles northeast of Marietta, they were joined by Judge Newt Morris. By daybreak they had reached Frey's Gin, two miles east of Marietta. Although they had claimed they were going to hang Leo over Mary's grave, they had probably planned to hang him in this spot from the beginning. It was owned by Sheriff Frey, one of the group's organizers, so they wouldn't be disturbed. Sheriff Frey had, in fact, tied the noose himself. And the location faced the house where Mary Phagan had been born and lived until her mother moved the family to Atlanta.

The lynchers led Leo to an oak tree. One of them later said that "he behaved throughout with a calmness and dignity and an utter lack of panic." While one of the men brought up a table and looped the hanging rope over a branch of the tree, Leo asked permission to write to Lucille. Someone gave him pencil and paper, and he wrote a brief note in a language the men didn't recognize. Some thought it was Yiddish, but it may have been German. No one knows the contents of that note to this day.

According to the lynchers, Leo said, "I think more of my wife and my mother than I do of my own life." His lynchers believed he meant that he thought so highly of the women in his life that he would not shame them by confessing to murder. But perhaps he meant that he honored them because they had consistently believed in his innocence and had not abandoned him, and their love and loyalty was worth more than whatever happened to him. Or he might simply have meant that he loved his wife and mother and was able to face his death knowing he had been a good husband and son.

The lynchers tied Leo's feet, lifted him onto the table, and wrapped a piece of cloth around his lower body, since he was only wearing the nightshirt. Leo's last request was that they return his wedding ring to Lucille.

At 7:05 A.M., Judge Newt Morris repeated the sentence of the court that Leo should be hanged by the neck until dead. Then the judge kicked the table out from under him.

Leo did not die immediately, because the fall from the table was not great enough to snap his neck. Instead, he suffocated over some minutes, struggling so desperately that the slash in his neck opened and he bled onto his shirt. Confident that their job was done, the lynchers drove away from the scene, leaving Sheriff Frey to find the body later. Deputy Sheriff Hicks (one of the lynchers) received a phone call with the official notification.

More than a thousand people swarmed to the scene within hours, eager for a sight of Leo's body—many eager for photographs and souvenirs as well. The atmosphere was somewhere between celebration, vindication, and religious rapture. The crowd swelled to three thousand, and its rowdier members wanted to rip the body down and desecrate it.

Aware of this possibility, Judge Morris returned to the scene to prevent any violence. He was afraid that such impassioned attacks on the body might undo the dignity of his group's lynching, which he viewed as the most appropriate way to carry out the jury's verdict, given the circumstances. Robert Howell, a rowdy hothead who wished he had been included in the lynching party, shouted at Leo's body, "You won't murder any more little innocent girls! We've got you now!!"

Leo Frank was lynched on the morning of August 16, 1915

LEO M. FRANK LYNCHED FOR CRIMINAL ASSAULT ON LITTLE MARY PHAGAN, NEAR MARIETTA, GEORGIA, 1915

Frank's death brought with it a business in souvenirs to commemorate the lynching, including postcards (*above and at left*). The card on the left reads "Leo M. Frank lynched for criminal assault on little Mary Phagan, near Marietta, Georgia, 1915."

Judge Morris tried to calm him down while the undertaker's men drove up, but someone sliced through the rope and Leo's body fell to the ground. As if waiting for that signal, Howell and the crowd pressed in upon him. Roger Winter wrote in the *Journal*, "Again and again, as a man grinds the head of a snake under his heel, did the man drive his heel into the face of Leo M. Frank, grinding the black hair into the dirt and dead black leaves until the crowd, stricken silent and motionless, could hear the man's heel as it made a crunching sound."

Finally, Judge Morris was able to stop Howell and remove the body. But the undertaker's wagon barely made it to Marietta's city limits before it was chased down by several cars. Fortunately, one of them was the judge's. He snatched the body and placed it in his back seat while his driver sped away from Marietta toward Atlanta. By the next day, picture postcards of Leo's body hanging from the noose, as well as cut pieces from his shirt and from the rope, were selling so fast that the police announced, "Any person selling articles represented as souvenirs of the lynching of Leo Frank must have a city license."

People across the nation were outraged. John Slaton said, "Every man who engaged in the lynching should be hanged, for he is an assassin."

Heartbroken, Lucille brought Leo's body to Brooklyn where an undertaker would try to rebuild Leo's ruined face. Reporters attempted to question the family, but Leo's mother said simply, "My son belongs to me. I want a quiet funeral." The private funeral was held at Mount Carmel Cemetery on Friday morning, August 20, 1915. Leo's mother cried out several times for her boy during the ceremony, and Lucille wept for her "angel" and nearly stumbled at the cemetery.

Back in Marietta, the Knights of Mary Phagan were congratulated in print by Tom Watson, although officials vowed to find the lynchers. Governor Harris pledged to do everything in his power "to see to it that the members of this mob receive fitting punishment for their crime." But no one turned in a single man. According to the *New York Times*, "The word mob does not seem descriptive, for these men did not display the ordinary characteristics of a mob. Lynching mobs are usually composed of riff-raff, but this one consisted of leading citizens of the community, men prominent in business and social circles."

Pallbearers carry Leo Frank's coffin in New York.

A Cobb County grand jury claimed they could not indict anyone for the lynching because they were unable to identify anyone connected with it. Seven members of the lynching party sat on the grand jury panel.

Not one of the lynchers would ever be arrested or punished, and none would even be publicly identified until decades later.

In the wake of Leo's lynching, his supporters were more vocal than ever. It was too late to help Leo, but it was high time to ensure that such injustice never happened to another Jew. The American Jewish Committee worked with other supporters to form the Jewish Anti-Defamation League of B'nai B'rith, which exists to this day. The group's mandate is to fight anti-Semitism and all forms of bigotry, defend democratic ideals, and protect civil rights in the United States and abroad.

Unfortunately, Leo's detractors became more vocal than ever as well. Invigorated by Watson's praise and his rhetoric condemning Jews, Catholics, and African Americans, the Knights of Mary Phagan reestablished the Ku Klux Klan. Originally formed during Reconstruction to intimidate Yankees and freed blacks, the Klan had become increasingly violent until many southerners joined federal authorities in calling for it to be shut down. This 1915 revitalization of the organization lasted considerably longer than the original Klan and was more violent. It became so powerful in the South that it almost took control of the Democratic Party in 1924. Watson proudly supported the Klan, claiming that in Georgia he was "the King of the Ku Klux."

Ironically, it was the family of some of these Klansmen who finally revealed the identity of the men who had lynched Leo Frank. For years, their names remained a well-known secret—well known in that everyone in Marietta knew who they were but secret in that no one in the legal system could identify them. But in the 1990s, Mary Phagan's great-grandniece made a list of the lynchers. She based it on information spontaneously volunteered by people who told her, when they found out who she was, that their father or grandfather or uncle had been among the group. Mary Phagan Kean's list appeared on the Internet on January 1, 2000—without her knowledge or consent.

Long before that happened, however, Lucille herself had died. She had returned to Atlanta to be with her parents after her husband's funeral. There, as the lynchers had promised, she was given Leo's wedding ring. One of them delivered it to a newspaperman, who brought it to her.

Lucille lived the rest of her life in Atlanta, maintaining that Leo was innocent. Until her death in 1957, she signed her name proudly as Mrs. Leo M. Frank.

Frank's lynching led to the reemergence of the Ku Klux Klan (*above*) and the founding of the Anti-Defamation League (*left*), two of the most important groups in the history of twentieth-century civil rights.

"LIES HEAPED ON LIES"

THE LAST EYEWITNESS

On March 6, 1982, nearly seventy years after Mary Phagan's murder, the last eyewitness signed an affidavit and prepared to return with it to Atlanta. Alonzo Mann, the office boy who had cried back in 1913 when he brought Leo the newspaper announcing his forthcoming arrest, stated:

> *In 1913 I was the office boy for Leo M. Frank, who ran the National Pencil Company. That was the year Leo Frank was convicted of the murder of Mary Phagan. I was fourteen years old at the time. I was called on as a witness in the murder trial. At that time I was put on the witness stand, but I did not tell all that I knew. I was not asked questions about what I knew. I did not volunteer. If I had revealed all I knew it would have cleared Leo Frank and would have saved his life.*

Alonzo Mann at the time of his affidavit in 1982.

Alonzo went on to describe his work at the pencil factory and then said that when his mother hadn't shown up to meet him before the parade on Confederate Memorial Day, he'd decided to go back to work. In a tone reminiscent of the shock and fear he must have felt when he was fourteen, the eighty-three-year-old man continued:

> Inside the door, I walked toward the stairwell. I looked to my right and I was confronted by a scene I will remember vividly until the day I die.
>
> Jim Conley was standing between the trapdoor that led to the basement and the elevator shaft. I have an impression that the trapdoor was partially open, but my eyes were fixed on Jim Conley.
>
> He had the body of Mary Phagan in his arms. I didn't know it was Mary Phagan. I only knew it was a girl.
>
> At that moment I couldn't tell if she was alive. She appeared to be unconscious. . . .
>
> Jim Conley turned around toward me. He either heard my footsteps coming or he sensed I was behind him. He wheeled on me and in a voice that was low but threatening and frightening to me, he said:
>
> "If you ever mention this I'll kill you."
>
> I turned and took a step or two—possibly three or four steps—up toward the second floor, but I . . . was fearful that the office might be closed, so I turned back toward Conley. I wanted to get out of there quick. He got to within eight feet of me. He reached out as if to put one arm or hand on me. I ran out of the front door and raced away from that building.
>
> I related to my mother what I had seen there at the pencil factory. She insisted that I not get involved. She told me to remain silent. My mother loved me. She knew Conley had threatened to kill me. She didn't want our family's name to be involved in controversy or for me to be subjected to any publicity. My father supported her in

telling me to remain silent. My mother repeated to me
over and over not to tell. She never thought Leo Frank
would be convicted. Of course, she was wrong. . . .
  Leo Frank was convicted by lies heaped on lies. It
wasn't just Conley who lied. . . .
  At last I am able to get this off my heart.
  I believe it will help people to understand that courts
and juries make mistakes. They made a mistake in the
Leo Frank case.

Jim Conley had already admitted to carrying Mary's body to the basement, but he had said he'd done so on Leo Frank's orders and with Leo's help. He'd also claimed that they had taken the body from the second floor to the basement in the elevator. Alonzo's testimony placed Jim Conley on the first floor without Leo, carrying Mary's body by himself. Alonzo also swore he had seen Conley taking Mary's body toward the trapdoor and the steps that led down to the basement, not riding down in the elevator with the body. These were two huge discrepancies in Jim Conley's stories that could have exonerated Leo and convicted the sweeper.

Alonzo's uncertainty about whether Mary was already dead or still alive matched the point raised during Leo's many appeals, that there were "cinders and saw-dust in Mary Phagan's nose and mouth, drawn in in the act of breathing." If Jim Conley had knocked Mary unconscious when she came down the stairs and refused to give him any of her pay, then thrown her down to the basement and murdered and robbed her there, then she would indeed have had sawdust and cinders in her airway. If Leo had murdered her outside his office as the State of Georgia had argued, then her airway would have been clean. Alonzo Mann submitted to two separate polygraph tests to confirm that he was telling the truth. He passed them both.

On the basis of this new testimony, the American Jewish Committee, the Atlanta Jewish Federation, and the Anti-Defamation League applied for a pardon from the Georgia State Board of Pardons and Paroles. While there was considerable sympathy from many

Mary Phagan — Jim Conley — Alonzo Mann — The Lynching — Leo Frank

SUNDAY, March 7, 1982
A GANNETT NEWSPAPER

THE TENNESSEAN

Special News Section

An Innocent Man Was Lynched

By FRANK RITTER,
JERRY THOMPSON
and ROBERT SHERBORNE
Copyright 1982, The Tennessean

LEO Frank, convicted in 1913 and lynched in 1915 in one of the most notorious murder cases in American history, was innocent, according to a sworn statement given by a witness in the case.

The testimony used to convict Frank was perjured, and the real killer of 14-year-old Mary Phagan was the man who gave that false testimony, the witness has disclosed to *The Tennessean*.

ALONZO MANN OF Bristol, Va., is the witness. Now 83 and ailing with a heart condition, he was Frank's office boy in 1913 at the National Pencil Co. factory in Atlanta. It was there on Confederate Memorial Day in April that little Mary Phagan was slain when she went to collect the $1.20 she was owed for 10 hours of work the previous Monday.

"Leo Frank did not kill Mary Phagan," Mann said. "She was murdered instead by Jim Conley."

Mann's memory is not perfect when he is recalling people, places and events of nearly 70 years ago. But he remembers vividly the confrontation with Jim Conley, who had the limp form of Mary Phagan in his arms.

Mary's battered body was found face down on a pile of sawdust

Interpretation of the confrontation between Alonzo Mann, then 14, and Jim Conley, holding the limp form of an on the first floor of National Pencil Co.
—Drawing by Pat Mitchell

13 Words Shook History

By SANDRA ROBERTS

JURY foreman F.E. Winburn had no way of knowing that the 13 words he was about to utter would unleash the moral fiber of this country and change American history forever.

"We the jury," Winburn said of Leo Frank, "find the defendant guilty of the murder of Mary Phagan."

The verdict comprised one simple sentence. It was delivered in the same antiseptic manner as dozens of other verdicts in Atlanta that year.

Yet Winburn's words were to be heard and debated around the world. They were to:
- Kindle rebirth of the Ku Klux Klan.
- Spark formation of the Anti-Defamation League of B'nai B'rith.
- Reform this country's laws governing the fair trial of criminal defendants.
- Alter the course and climate of Georgia politics for decades.

Ironically, the stage on which these three turns of history — Leo M. Frank — died quietly. In the end, he wanted to die with dignity, to take time and not make noise, lynched from an oak tree in Marietta, Ga.

Two months after the lynching, a Ku Klux Klan cross — to one side to burn this hate — was raised atop nearby Stone Mountain, outside Atlanta.

WILLIAM J SIMMONS, a former clergyman, led the Klansmen. He had driven them from the ruins of a secret order known as the Knights of Mary Phagan. This secret order's avowed purpose was to avenge Mary Phagan's death.

After the lynching this purpose had been fulfilled. But the vengeance which spawned the organization continued, and Simmons was able to tap the simmering disquiet, to channel it into another organization — the Ku Klux Klan.

Encouraged by his men, with which they escaped punishment for lynching Leo Frank, many of the Knights of Mary Phagan were eager to join him.

SIMMONS WAS NAMED the new leader of the new founded Empire of the Knights of the Ku Klux Klan — an organization with offshoots which flourish today under several names, promoting racial and religious hatred.

When first organized after the Civil War, the Klan had been opposed primarily to blacks and carpetbaggers. But the new Klansmen, as organized by Simmons, expanded their hatred to include Jews and Catholics. Their targets now became, temporarily for the most part.

Contemporaneously with the rebirth of the Klan, American Jews came to realize, as the never had before, how deeply they were the objects of hate and loathing even in the United States. Middle-class Jews were well entrenched in business, and although they were innocent socially and politically from the Gentile population, they nonetheless felt the sting of anti-Semitism.

BEFORE FRANK's arrest and conviction, anti-Semitism was more around than most in the United States. Middle-class Jews were well entrenched in business, and although they were insulated socially and politically from the Gentile

mainstream, there was little evidence of overt prejudice.

But Frank's trial crystallized the feelings against Gentile's underlying hatred and fear of the Jew. The stench of "crucify the Jew's neck" and "damned sheeny" that were heard in the courtroom derided Jews throughout the world that Frank's religion was a substantive factor in the case.

American Jews were hard to reach. They had examined the details of the Frank case and were convinced of his innocence. Equally important was the Jewish holding that Jews must come to the aid of their distressed brethren.

HOWEVER, THE American Jewish community was divided on the best method for aiding Frank. The president of the American Jewish Committee, New York attorney Louis Marshall, was hesitant about having that organization champion openly the cause of a convicted Jewish boy.

The Marshall's Jewish allies helped Frank in a number of subtle ways. Marshall, a renowned constitutional lawyer, represented him before the U.S. Supreme Court. Chicago advertising magnate Albert Lasker contributed more than $100,000 to the Frank legal fund and took a year's leave from his business to direct a vast investigation and amass additional funds. Other prominent Jews urged caution, fearing that the Frank case, and disloyal to political figures and business interests to the Jewish population.

Jews in Georgia were openly antagonistic to the aftermath of the Frank trial. After the canonization of his death sentence, Jews were regarded by Frank's home town, Jews left the city for good; others were forced on some accusations that they had borrowed and become their business, with wives and children who were put on trial and suspected of being the mass murderer who terrorized Atlanta for months.

LEO FRANK's LYNCHING made it painfully obvious that Jews — as well as blacks — were subject to hanging by the mob. After Frank's lynching and the Frank lynching, had the 5,000 Jews in Georgia left the state.

The Jews who remained in Atlanta were chastised literally for a massive boycott of Jewish businesses. In one instance several Jewish merchants were forced to abandon their establishments, with wives and children fearful of the emotional hysteria which terrorized Atlanta for months.

THE ADL, AIDED by the NAACP, became vigorous in opposing all lynchings. To this day the group's purpose is to correct falsehoods in all forms of media, and to distribute accurate information about

Judaism. It owes its genesis to Leo Frank.

Another historical aspect of the case has to do with the administration of justice in this country.

For Frank's attorneys brought to the U.S. Supreme Court, for the first time, the question of whether a criminal defendant can get a fair, impartial trial if the jurors during the case are affected by mass prejudice.

Frank's attorneys argued to the high court that the spectators at Frank's trial and the mobs outside the courtroom frightened the jurors so badly that the jury members were afraid to acquit him.

THE SUPREME COURT, however, by a 7-2 vote, rejected this argument and upheld Frank's conviction.

Frank dissenting Justice Oliver Wendell Holmes in a dissent joined by Justice Charles Evans Hughes, said such a coerced jury atmosphere makes a fair trial impossible.

"Mob law does not become the process of law by securing the assent of a terrorized jury," Holmes wrote.

...

(Continued From Page 1)

An Innocent Man Was Lynched

remain silent. Later, Frank was lynched by a mob from Marietta, Ga. I knew, of course, that because I kept silent Leo Frank lost his life.

"I HAVE SPENT many nights thinking about that I have assured to live with it.

"At last I am able to get this off my heart. I believe it will help people to understand that prejudice and injustice can make mistakes."

Mann first told his story to Tennessean reporter Jerry Thompson. Over a period of several weeks he repeated it many times to a team of Tennessean staff members including reporter Robert Sherborne. The reporters and the Tennessean also interviewed Sandra Roberts, then began a thorough investigation of the Mary Phagan-Leo Frank case, checking the information which Mann had given to see whether it disclosed the facts of the case.

Almost Mann's story a vastly important because it narrows history — and it also makes history. Many legal scholars and writers who have researched the case have come away convinced that Frank was innocent, but a major chain of anti-social event in Atlanta in 1913.

And many who have examined the case have suspected that it was Jim Conley who murdered Mary Phagan. At least three persons later were pointed as saying he confessed to them he was the killer.

Researchers and scholars have speculated in books and articles over the years as to how the murder might have occurred.

BUT MANN HAS always been lacking has been that crucial piece of evidence — the eye-witness account to refute Conley. Mann's testimony today, combined in a sworn affidavit accompanying this story, provides that vital evidence.

Mann will be a witness for the defense at the trial of Frank, but he was never called to sit on the stand or he returned, and he did not testify for Frank because it was to testify for him. But did he tell anything else that he knew of the crime?

Had he spoken out then, the course of history as the frank could have been dramatically different.

The aftermath of that crime shocked the region.

THE MURDER OF Mary Phagan and the trial of the men accused of killing her had immediate consequences. Members of the mob that lynched Frank were active in the rebirth of the Ku Klux Klan. The wave of anti-Semitism which swept the South as a result of the case led to creation of the Anti-Defamation League of B'nai B'rith.

The chief prosecutor in the Frank case, Hugh

Dorsey, was elected governor; Tom Watson, whose newspaper condemned Frank as "a Jew Sodomite," was elected to the U.S. Senate. Gov. Slaton was exiled in political obscurity.

It all started with Mary Phagan's slaying.

ATLANTA POLICE, under extreme pressure to solve the case, arrested Leo Frank of having murdered Mary Phagan. He was implied as the motive.

The evidence was flimsy and circumstantial — except for the detailed testimony of the prosecution's chief witness, Jim Conley.

Frank, 29, was from New York and was Jewish — a Yankee Jew. Georgians, in the main, disliked Northerners and distrusted Jews. During the trial, hundreds of people gathered in the street outside and shouted, and there were frequent periods of "Kill the Jew!"

The families of Mary Phagan, like many others in Georgia, had moved to Atlanta from the farm to seek a better life. In those days it was not unusual for a girl to go to work in Atlanta at an early age, and Mary, like millions of other young workers in Georgia, turned many trusted in the mills.

MARY WAS A BEAUTIFUL girl — 4 feet 8 inches tall and weighing about 100 pounds. She had long, reddish-blond hair that hung down her back when it was not brushed.

The community was outraged by her murder. In the dead race anonymous, a brutal murder of a member of Southern womanhood.

Many saw the trial of Mary Phagan as the symbol of ravished womanhood. Jim Frank became a symbol of all that was perceived to be wrong with the South in 1913 — vast and perversion, greed and exploitation.

BEFORE ATLANTA police finally decided on Frank as their prime suspect, they arrested and other persons, including Conley, in connection with the murder. In retrospect, it appears investigators ignored evidence which pointed compellingly toward Conley's guilt.

Scholars who have studied the events of 1913 in Atlanta have tried to figure out why this happened. Some have theorized they found the answer in the words of the late Luther Otterbein Bricker, pastor of First Christian Church in Bellwood, Ga., who was Mary Phagan's minister. Some 30 years after her death, in a letter to a friend, Bricker wrote:

"When the police arrested Leo, and a Yankee Jew at that, all of the inborn prejudice against Jews rose up in a feeling of satisfaction, that here was a Jew to put in a manner of satisfaction, that here

would be a victim worthy to pay for the crime. From that day on, the newspapers were filled with the most awful stories, affidavits and testimonies, which proved the guilt of Leo M. Frank beyond the shadow of a doubt.

"THE POLICE GOT prostitutes and criminals on whom they had something, to swear anything and everything they wanted them to swear to. And reading these stories in the paper day by day, there was no doubt in the mind of the general public but that Frank was guilty. And the whole city was in a frenzy. We were all against him as a blood thirsty. Frank was brought to trial in mob spirit. Our could feel the waves of madness which swept us all."

In Frank was convicted. The court sentenced him to hang. His numerous appeals wound their way through the courts for another two years.

"The condemnation of his statements to the prison by Hugh Gov. Slaton Once this bottom exploitation of Slaton's term of office, It was an act of amazing courage. By so, in convict in Georgia. Almost every Georgia townsman had a high school sweetheart, and mob businessmen and bed believe murdered up there and millions, home hall permanently from the jail community.

At one point a crowd of some 5,000 persons armed with revolvers, rifles, saws, hatchets and dynamite, surrounded the governor's mansion. They were routed by the state militia before they could do harm to Slaton.

WITHIN DAYS OF the announcement of the commutation order, a group of about 25 men, calling themselves the Knights of Mary Phagan, met at the site of the little girl's grave and vowed to avenge her death. Twenty-five of them were picked to start vengeance against Frank.

Late one night a group of armed men, 25 vigilantes stormed the prison farm at Milledgeville, where Frank was being held. From there they took him away to Marietta — to the place where Mary Phagan grew up, and drove 175 miles to an oak grove just outside Marietta, within a stone's fathom of where Mary Phagan was born.

They hanged Frank's body from a limb and cut hanged him from an oak branch facing in the direction of the Phagan home.

NO ONE WAS EVER arrested for the lynching of Leo Frank. A grand jury, called to investigate the case, failed to indict anyone. Tom Watson, a formidable political figure, who controlled the populist movement in the state to preserve the head of Jews, Catholics and blacks, wrote to his friends:

"In putting the festival murderer to death, the

Vigilance Committee has done what the Sheriff would have done if Slaton had not been elected, and would have done if Slaton had not been governor ... LET JEW LIBERTARIAN TAKE NOTICE! Conley is not the cause of his criminals."

The Mary Phagan-Leo Frank case was over. The murder had been avenged and that was the end of it, so some thought at the time.

BUT IT WAS NOT OVER. Today, nearly 70 years later, the case still lives.

"I believe in the sight of God that Jim Conley killed Mary Phagan, not Leo Frank, and not Alonzo Mann, who has brought the case back to life.

"There will be some people who will be angry at me because I kept all this silent until it was too late to save Leo Frank's life. They will say that lynch prejudice and injustice will make another. The only thing I can say is that she did what my mother told me to do.

"Other people may hate me for telling it. I hope not, but I am prepared for that, too. I know that I haven't a long time to live. All that I have said is the truth.

"While my time comes, I hope that God under stands me better for having told it. That is what matters most."

(Turn to Page 2, Column 1)

Blindfolded and handcuffed, Leo Frank is lynched from an oak tree in Marietta, Ga., Aug. 17, 1915.
— Courtesy of the Georgia State Archives

This graph from a psychological stress evaluation, given to Alonzo Mann indicates he was telling the truth when he was asked: "Do this (Confederate Memorial) Day shortly after noon did you see Jim Conley holding a girl in his arms that looked like Mary Phagan?" — and, "When you saw Jim Conley holding Mary in his arms did you threaten to kill you?"

JUSTICE BETRAYED
a sin of silence

- Page 7
An analysis of the evidence implicating Jim Conley.

- Page 8
A chronology of the Phagan-Frank case.
Lonnie Mann's incomplete testimony at Leo Frank's trial.
The impact of a book by Harry Golden on the Phagan-Frank case.

- Page 9
Alonzo Mann's sworn affidavit.

- Page 10
Georgia Gov. John Slaton — a "profile in courage."
Nashville Mayor Hillary H. Howse's letter urging leniency for Frank.
The Phagan-Frank case — a boon to newspaper circulation.

southerners for this request, some Georgians argued passionately against it. Former Georgia Court of Appeals judge Randall Evans insisted the evidence against Leo Frank had been overwhelming. He attacked Governor Slaton's commutation as a "rape of the judicial process" and said the request for a posthumous pardon was "completely ridiculous."

Although the board considered this application, the members were limited in how much research they could actually do into the original case. Hugh Dorsey had diligently saved all of his notes and even the forensic evidence from his most famous case, but his records disappeared shortly after his death in 1948. On December 22, 1983, despite Alonzo's appearance in person before the state board, the application was rejected on the grounds that it did not prove Leo's innocence.

Alonzo died in March of 1985, but the Anti-Defamation League filed a new application for pardon. Members of the board were troubled that the case had never fully been resolved because Leo had been lynched before he was able to make further efforts to prove his innocence. They also admitted that the State of Georgia had failed to protect the prisoner in its care. On March 11, 1986, the board issued a final statement, concluding:

> *Without attempting to address the question of guilt or innocence, and in recognition of the state's failure to protect the person of Leo M. Frank and thereby preserve his opportunity for continued legal appeal of his conviction, and in recognition of the state's failure to bring his killers to justice, the State Board of Pardons and Paroles, in compliance with its constitutional and statutory authority, hereby grants to Leo M. Frank a pardon.*

Neither the board nor any court was ever able to consider the possibility that Jim Conley was the sole murderer, as Alonzo Mann, William Smith, Will Green, Governor Slaton, and even Judge Roan ultimately believed. After Conley served his one-year sentence for accessory, he spent the rest of his life in and out of prison, finally disappearing in the 1960s and presumed dead. In 1959 attorney A. L. Henson published his memoirs and claimed that while Jim Conley had been his client, the man had confessed to him that he had struggled with a girl in the pencil factory but had then blanked out. When Conley came to himself, he was in the basement and the girl was dead. Henson had not spoken out earlier because of lawyer-client privilege.

Some passionate analysts of the case continue to vehemently argue Conley's guilt versus Leo's guilt. Mary Phagan's great-grandniece, Mary Phagan Kean, still insists that Leo "is not a martyr, he is a murderer." But most people on both sides agree that Leo never got a fair trial. Even with the perspective of many decades of elapsed time, however, many people remain unsure of what really happened. A number of them have written their own versions of the story in their struggle to explore this troubling case and find its truths.

Ward Greene was the first of several writers to tackle the case in his 1936 novel, *Death in the Deep South*. In the late 1930s, *They Won't Forget* opened in movie theaters, and in 1988, a television miniseries aired written by Larry McMurtry, called *The Murder of Mary Phagan*. This film still turns up occasionally on cable channels. In 2000 playwright Alfred Uhry and composer-lyricist Jason Robert Brown wrote a musical for Broadway about the case, called *Parade*. And in 2009, Ben Loeterman's documentary titled *The People v. Leo Frank* aired on PBS with a world premiere in Cobb County, where Leo was lynched. All of these writers agree that Leo Frank did not get a fair trial. They have all tried to make sense out of what happened to Mary and Leo, yet questions persist.

Did the jury convict Leo Frank on the basis of the evidence? Or was public opinion prejudiced against Leo because he was a Jewish, college-educated, well-paid Yankee who had come into this southern city on the wave of northern industrialization? Would his fate have been the same if he had been an Atlanta Jew instead of a Yankee Jew? Did he pay with his Yankee blood for the devastation of Atlanta at the hands of William T. Sherman during the "Recent Unpleasantness"? Or was Leo Frank convicted by the anti-Semitic sentiment that ran so strong during his trial? How far will good citizens go down the path toward violence because they hate people who belong to a particular religion or ethnic group?

Perhaps the most troubling question is why so many people involved in the case lied, particularly so many factory employees. They admitted they lied, and some said they were persuaded or even coerced by Hugh Dorsey, but what about the others? Was it merely because they liked the idea of so many people paying attention to them and respecting them? Did they give in to peer pressure? Were they caught up in some sort of emotional mass hysteria? Did they even convince themselves that they were telling the truth or perhaps that their lies were unimportant because surely Leo Frank was guilty or he wouldn't be in court? Whatever the reason, some of them were never able to let go of their belief that Mary Phagan's killer had, indeed, been hanged in Marietta.

That mass hysteria or prejudice or delusion continued to grip Atlanta even after World War I. In 1922 journalist Pierre Van Paassen tried to publish the fact that the photos of the bite marks on Mary's shoulder did not match the photos taken of Leo's teeth and that Dorsey had known but suppressed the information to get a conviction. Van Paassen received a note warning him to "lay off the Frank case if you want to keep healthy."

Van Paassen realized how deeply sentiments still ran one morning when a "large automobile drove up alongside of me and forced me into the track of a fast-moving streetcar coming from the opposite direction. My car was demolished, but I escaped." Seven years had passed since Leo's lynching, and World War I had changed the face of the world more than Mary Phagan's friends at the factory could have imagined, yet many citizens of Atlanta still refused to consider that the evidence that convicted Leo Frank was a tissue of lies and innuendo.

Significant changes have been made in the U.S. legal system since Leo was convicted. For example, if prosecutors discover exculpatory evidence that suggests the accused is innocent, such as the forensic evidence of the hair found near Leo's office or the identification of the bite marks, they are required to share that evidence with the defense under the rules of discovery. But not all prosecutors follow the rules, even today. Sometimes they believe so strongly that someone is guilty that they suppress evidence that might get in the way of convincing a jury to convict the suspect. Or sometimes they abuse the system to advance their personal careers. How can a suspect offer a defense if the system that protects his or her rights has been corrupted?

Atlanta's Mayor Woodward called Leo's lynching for Mary Phagan's murder "a just penalty for an unspeakable crime." But was Mary's murder the only unspeakable crime? Wasn't Leo's lynching an unspeakable crime also? What about the lies of so many teenage witnesses? Or Alonzo Mann's silence? Or the way the entire case perverted the U.S. concept of justice?

It's hard to be certain whether it would have made a difference if Alonzo had ignored his mother and spoken out at Leo Frank's trial. Perhaps Dorsey would merely have woven the eyewitness account into his argument, claiming that the boy had seen only the large African American man carrying the body and not noticed the smaller white man behind him. The fact that he had not told the truth haunted Alonzo all his life, although he said he tried to tell people a few times and was always told not to raise the specter of the old case again.

"I was only 14 years old," Alonzo told reporters in 1982. "Nowadays you're practically a man at that age. But things were different then. . . . I was just a boy. I was scared. I knew that if Jim Conley got his hands on me, he would have killed me." If fourteen was young enough to be fearful of the consequences of his actions and to feel he must obey his mother, even though that meant lying on the witness stand, Alonzo was sixteen by the time Governor Slaton investigated the verdict. How old do you have to be to make up your mind whether or not to speak out, despite what your parents tell you and regardless of the consequences?

To weigh the issues in the case of Mary Phagan's murder and Leo Frank's lynching is to look deep into the darker side of the U.S.: the painful injustice of the nation's "justice" system; the bitter resentment of history's memory; the outrage of ambition; the stark realities of racial, religious, and geographic prejudice; and the fear that standing against society's wrongs will demand too high a cost to pay. At the same time, it is impossible to look at this case and not also see the tender loyalty of Leo's wife; the admiration of his lawyers and friends; and the determination of so many legal minds to overturn his conviction, simply because they could not stand by and witness such injustice. In the end, perhaps the final verdict on this case must be, as Governor John Slaton said, a matter of conscience.

In this day of fading ideals and
disappearing land marks, little Mary Phagan's
heroism is an heirloom, than which there is
nothing more precious among the old red hills
of Georgia.

Sleep, little girl; sleep in your humble
grave but if the angels are good to you in the
realms beyond the trouble sunset and the
clouded stars, they will let you know that
many an aching heart in Georgia beats for you,
and many a tear, from eyes unused to weep,
has paid you a tribute too sacred for words.

—Mary Phagan's epitaph on her tombstone
(donated by Tom Watson)

Leo Frank (1884–1915)
Wrongly accused, Falsely convicted,
Wantonly murdered
Pardoned, 1986
Remembered on the 80th yahrzeith, 1995/5755
By the Jewish Community of Cobb County

—private marker at the site
of Leo Frank's lynching

MAJOR FIGURES IN THE LEO FRANK CASE

LEO FRANK AND FAMILY

Leo M. Frank: twenty-nine-year-old superintendent of the National Pencil Company; accused of murdering Mary Phagan

Lucille Frank: Leo Frank's wife

Moses Frank: Leo Frank's uncle; owner of the National Pencil Company

Rachel and Rudolph Frank: Leo Frank's parents

Emil and Josephine Selig: Lucille Frank's parents, in whose home Leo and Lucille Frank lived

MARY PHAGAN AND FAMILY

Frannie Coleman: Mary Phagan's mother

John W. Coleman: Mary Phagan's stepfather

Mary Phagan: thirteen-year-old worker at the National Pencil Company; murdered at the factory on April 26, 1913

ATTORNEYS AND OFFICERS OF THE COURT

Henry Alexander: handwriting analyst and defense attorney for Leo Frank

Reuben Arnold: defense attorney for Leo Frank

Paul Donehoo: Fulton County coroner; conducted Mary Phagan's inquest

Hugh Dorsey: Atlanta's solicitor general; prosecuted the case against Leo Frank

Herbert Haas: defense attorney for Leo Frank; corporate attorney for the National Pencil Company

Henry Harris: secretary of the Georgia Board of Health; conducted autopsy of Mary Phagan's body

J. W. Hurt: Fulton County medical examiner; participated in autopsy of Mary Phagan's body

Louis Marshall: attorney and president of the American Jewish Committee; took Leo Frank's case before the Supreme Court

Leonard S. Roan: judge; presided over Leo Frank's murder trial

Luther Z. Rosser: defense attorney for Leo Frank

William Smith: attorney for Jim Conley

INVESTIGATORS

James Litchfield Beavers: Atlanta police chief

John Black: police detective; first to question Leo Frank

Newport Lanford: chief of detectives in Atlanta's police department

W. W. "Boots" Rogers: police officer

Harry Scott: Pinkerton detective

John Starnes: police detective

POLITICIANS

John M. Slaton: governor of Georgia

Tom Watson: Georgia politician; published anti-Semitic magazines and worked against Leo Frank and his supporters

NATIONAL PENCIL COMPANY EMPLOYEES AND ASSOCIATES

Robert Barrett: eighteen-year-old factory worker; discovered evidence in the metal department

Jim Conley: janitor; prosecution's star witness against Leo Frank

Helen Ferguson: sixteen-year-old factory worker and close friend of Mary; testified for the prosecution

Dewey Hewell: sixteen-year-old former employee; testified for the prosecution but later said that she had been threatened and bribed for her testimony

Grace Hicks: seventeen-year-old worker; identified Mary's body

Magnolia Kennedy: fourteen-year-old worker; identified Mary's hair on lathe; testified for the defense

Newt Lee: night watchman; first suspect in the murder

Alonzo Mann: fourteen-year-old office boy

Lemmie Quinn: foreman

Herbert Schiff: assistant superintendent

Monteen Stover: fourteen-year-old worker; testified for the prosecution

OTHER MAJOR WITNESSES

Annie Maud Carter: inmate who received love letters from Jim Conley; testified that Conley confessed to her that he killed Mary

George Epps: fifteen-year-old newsboy; testified that Mary was afraid of Leo Frank

Will Green: carnival worker; claimed to have seen Jim Conley attack Mary

Minola McKnight: cook for the Seligs and Franks; gave police a statement against Leo Frank and then told reporters she had been forced to lie

William Mincey: insurance salesman; claimed Jim Conley told him he had killed a girl on the afternoon of Mary's murder

REPORTERS

Britt Craig: reporter for the *Atlanta Constitution*; accompanied police when they responded to initial report of Mary's murder

Harold Ross: reporter for the *Atlanta Journal*; removed from the police station notes found near Mary's body

TIMELINE

April 26, 1913   Mary Phagan is murdered on Confederate Memorial Day.

April 27, 1913   Mary Phagan's body is discovered. Newt Lee is arrested. Leo Frank is interrogated for the first time.

April 29, 1913   The funeral of Mary Phagan is held. Leo Frank is arrested.

April 30, 1913   Coroner's inquest begins.

May 1, 1913   Police arrest and release Jim Conley.

May 5, 1913   Mary Phagan's body is exhumed for autopsy.

May 7, 1913   Mary Phagan's body is exhumed a second time.

May 8, 1913   The inquest concludes.

May 18, 1913   Police question Jim Conley.

May 23, 1913   The grand jury indicts Leo Frank.

July 28, 1913   The trial of Leo Frank begins.

August 25, 1913   The jury returns a verdict of guilty.

August 26, 1913   Judge Leonard S. Roan sentences Leo Frank to hang for the murder of Mary Phagan.

October 31, 1913   Judge Roan denies a motion for a new trial.

February 17, 1914   Georgia Supreme Court denies a motion for a new trial.

February 24, 1914   Jim Conley is convicted of being an accessory after the fact to Mary Phagan's murder and sentenced to one year on a chain gang.

April 6, 1914   The defense files an extraordinary motion in Fulton County Superior Court and asks for a new trial on the basis of new evidence.

April 16, 1914   The defense files a motion in Fulton County Superior Court to set aside the original guilty verdict.

May 6, 1914   The Fulton County Superior Court denies a request for new trial. The defense appeals to Georgia Supreme Court.

June 6, 1914   The Georgia Supreme Court denies a motion to set aside the verdict. The defense appeals to the Georgia Supreme Court.

October 14, 1914   The Georgia Supreme Court denies appeal on extraordinary motion for a new trial.

November 17, 1914   The Georgia Supreme Court denies appeal to set aside the original guilty verdict.

December 7, 1914   U.S. Supreme Court denies a request for review of November 17 Georgia Supreme Court ruling.

December 9, 1914	Jim Conley is released.
December 17, 1914	The defense applies to the U.S. District Court for a writ of *habeas corpus.*
December 19, 1914	The District Court denies a writ of *habeas corpus.*
December 28, 1914	The U.S. Supreme Court agrees to hear arguments on the issue of due process.
February 23, 1915	Judge Leonard S. Roan dies of cancer.
February 25, 1915	The Supreme Court begins hearing arguments on Leo Frank's appeal.
April 9, 1915	The Supreme Court rejects the appeal.
May 10, 1915	Leo Frank's execution is rescheduled for June 22, 1915.
June 8, 1915	The Georgia Prison Commission denies petition for clemency.
June 20, 1915	Governor John Slaton commutes Frank's sentence to life in prison.
June 22, 1915	Armed mobs attack Governor Slaton's home.
July 17, 1915	Prisoner William Creen slashes Leo Frank's throat at Georgia State Prison Farm. Two prisoners, who are doctors, save Frank's life.
August 16, 1915	A mob of twenty-five armed men breaks into Georgia State Prison Farm and removes Leo Frank.
August 17, 1915	The lynch mob hangs Leo Frank, claiming to be carrying out the jury's verdict.
August 20, 1915	Leo Frank is buried in Brooklyn, New York.
September 2, 1915	The Cobb County grand jury fails to indict anyone for Leo Frank's lynching.
April 23, 1957	Lucille Frank dies in Atlanta.
March 6, 1982	Alonzo Mann signs an affidavit asserting Leo Frank's innocence and Jim Conley's guilt.
January 4, 1983	The Anti-Defamation League applies for a posthumous pardon for Leo Frank.
December 22, 1983	The Georgia Board of Pardons and Paroles denies the pardon.
March 19, 1985	Alonzo Mann dies.
March 11, 1986	The Georgia Board of Pardons and Paroles issues a pardon to Leo Frank, citing the state's failure to protect him while in custody or bring his killers to justice.
January 1, 2000	Atlanta librarian Stephen Goldfarb publishes the names on the Internet of Leo Frank's lynchers.

GLOSSARY OF LEGAL TERMINOLOGY

affidavit: a written declaration made under oath

appeal: an application to a higher court for a ruling or verdict to be reviewed and reversed

attorney-client privilege: a legal concept and the law in most of the United States that keeps all communications between a client and that person's attorney confidential

capital: punishable by death

chain of evidence: also called chain of custody; the careful handling and documentation of the whereabouts of all evidence in an investigation to ensure that evidence is not lost, contaminated, or tampered with

circumstantial evidence: evidence that indicates the possibility of guilt but does not directly prove it

clemency: mercy or leniency extended by a person in authority to a convict

commute: to change a sentence to a less severe one, such as a reduction of a death penalty sentence to life imprisonment

coroner: a government official whose job is to investigate deaths that are not clearly due to natural causes. This investigation takes place by means of an inquest.

counsel: a legal adviser such as an attorney or advice given by such a person

exculpatory evidence: evidence that tends to show that a defendant is not guilty

forensic evidence: evidence that is obtained by the use of scientific methods

grand jury: a group of citizens who are summoned to decide whether a person should be formally charged with a crime (indicted)

indict: to formally charge a person with a crime. An indictment leads to a trial to determine the guilt or innocence of the person charged.

inquest: a legal inquiry, held before a jury and led by a coroner, into a suspicious death

jury: a group of citizens who are summoned to make a decision in a legal proceeding

medical examiner: a physician appointed by the government to conduct autopsies on the bodies of people who have died under suspicious circumstances

motion: a request by an attorney for a judge to take a specific action in a legal proceeding

overrule: to reject, in the role of judge, the request of an attorney in a legal proceeding

overturn: to reverse the verdict of a lower court as the result of a successful appeal

pardon: to release a convicted person from penalty for an offense

solicitor general: a government official who prosecutes cases against accused criminals

subpoena: an official summons to appear as a witness in a legal proceeding

verdict: the decision of a jury regarding a legal matter in a trial, such as the guilt or innocence of a person charged with a crime

FURTHER READING

BOOKS

Carnes, Jim. *Us and Them: A History of Intolerance in America*. New York: Oxford University Press, 1996.
Read fourteen cases studies of intolerance in United States history, from colonial times through the twentieth century.

Cohen, Daniel. *Yellow Journalism: Scandal, Sensationalism, and Gossip in the Media*. Minneapolis: Twenty-First Century Books, 2000.
Learn about the history of yellow journalism in the United States and the effects of sensational media on public opinion.

Diner, Hasia R. *A New Promised Land: A History of Jews in America*. New York: Oxford University Press, 2003.
This book chronicles the history of Jewish life in America.

Dudley, William. *Mass Media*. Farmington Hills, MI: Greenhaven Press, 2005.
From the Opposing Viewpoints series, this book addresses controversial issues about mass media and the opposing sides of the debates.

Levine, Ellen S. *Catch a Tiger by the Toe*. New York: Viking, 2005.
In this historical novel set in the 1950s, a thirteen-year-old girl, whose father is tried as a Communist during the Red Scare, grapples with issues of social justice and civil rights.

Rossel, Seymour. *Let Freedom Ring: A History of the Jews in the United States*. West Orange, NJ: Behrman House, 1995.
Learn more about the history of Judaism and ethnic relations in the United States.

Sharenow, Robert. *My Mother the Cheerleader*. New York: Laura Geringer Books, 2007.
This novel tells a story of a fourteen-year-old girl whose mother pulls her out of her New Orleans school when the school is desegregated in 1960. It explores some of the religious, political, and race issues that existed in New Orleans.

WEBSITES

American Jewish Archives
http://www.americanjewisharchives.org
The American Jewish Archives houses historic photos and documents significant to the American Jewish experience. Follow the links to their online exhibit to view part of their collection.

Anti-Defamation League
http://www.adl.org/
The Anti-Defamation League website features news articles relating to anti-Semitism and civil rights issues.

Atlanta History Center
http://www.atlantahistorycenter.com
For a glimpse at Atlanta's history, explore the Atlanta History Center's photos of their exhibits.

William Breman Jewish Heritage and Holocaust Museum
http://www.thebreman.org/
This museum website has more information on the history of the Jewish community in Georgia, including a description of the museum's Leo Frank family document collection.

AUTHOR'S NOTE AND ACKNOWLEDGMENTS

To write a book like *An Unspeakable Crime* is to embark on a journey of research that amounts to a detective's following a trail of convoluted clues. One source leads to another and then backtracks to a third that tells you something more about the first. The journey started simply enough: in 1998 a friend of mine mentioned the Leo Frank case. He assured me that I would be interested because my husband often serves as an expert witness in murder conviction appeals, and I feel as strongly as he does about the problems with our justice system.

Taking my friend's advice, I read Leonard Dinnerstein's book, *The Leo Frank Case* (the most complete reference at the time, as Steve Oney would not publish his comprehensive book, *And the Dead Shall Rise,* until later in my research journey). I found that I could not get the case out of my mind. I listened to the score of *Parade*, and watched *The Murder of Mary Phagan* on cable, astonished that such a travesty of justice could have been allowed to occur.

The case stayed with me, and when I wrote my novel *The Perfect Shot,* I used a school history project about Leo Frank as the catalyst for my main character's change and growth. E-mails from readers told me that the case stayed with them too. It also stayed with my wonderful editor, Shannon Barefield, who has worked with me on many books. She encouraged me to consider writing a nonfiction book about it, and because I felt I still had so many unanswered questions, I agreed wholeheartedly.

I searched for source material and was further astounded that so little accurate published material could be found at that time. Several fictionalized accounts of the case had been published. Mary Phagan Kean (Mary Phagan's great-grandniece) had published a personal and passionate account of the murder from her family's perspective, and Harry Golden had published several accounts of the case from his Jewish perspective. But I couldn't find the answers I sought, and I discovered more complications than solutions. I wondered why quotations from the trial varied so widely, until I discovered that the original trial transcript had mysteriously disappeared from the courthouse. The only sources that survived were incomplete trial citations in the Brief of Evidence that was submitted during the appeals and published pamphlets containing edited versions of individual lawyers' arguments. I was also surprised that nothing about the case was available for teen readers, since it involved so many teenagers.

Material on the Internet can be unreliable, but I discovered the *Georgia Stories: History Online Project.* This was not a website consisting of someone's unvetted opinions but a site that had scans of actual letters and newspaper and magazine articles. Reading these made me realize that original material other than the trial transcript was out there, if I was willing to follow the trail. I lived in southern Indiana at the time, so I started with the newspaper articles, letters, diaries, and photographs in the Jacob Rader Marcus Center of the American Jewish Archives, in the Cincinnati Campus of the Hebrew Union College, Jewish

Institute of Religion. There Dorothy Smith, Vicki Lipski, Elise Nienaber, and Camille Servizzi helped me sort through the archives.

I read crumbling, orangey brown newspaper clippings with ragged edges that looked as if they had been chewed upon by time. Some were so brittle that they had broken along the fold lines. I listened to a taped interview of MacLellan Smith, a newspaperman who had sat in the courtroom during Leo Frank's original trial. I held letters that Leo had written to Lucille when they were first in love and letters written from the prison farm, and I saw how his handwriting changed from the slanted elegance of a confident businessman to the more rounded, penciled scrawl of an imprisoned convict. I looked at photographs of the lynching. I read Lucille's notes about nursing Leo after his throat was slashed and about her horror at his death. And I had to know more.

The Marcus Center collection mentioned materials at Emory University and the Atlanta History Center, and I was already aware of a collection at the Breman Jewish Heritage and Holocaust Museum. These are all located in Atlanta, so I headed there. In the Robert W. Woodruff Library in Atlanta, Kathy Shoemaker was glad to help me and encouraged me to photograph their collection. I read the *Tennessean's* articles about Alonzo Mann's 1982 bombshell, the published version of Hugh Dorsey's closing, newspaper clippings, and the transcripts of Governor Slaton's hearings. My fascination with Governor Slaton led me to his papers, preserved at the Georgia Archives, south of Atlanta in Morrow. Senior Archivist Dale Couch and Military Records Archivist Andy Phrydas were invaluable in bringing me Slaton's correspondence and clippings about his commutation order. I was particularly touched by the letter from Lucille, pleading her husband's case.

In the Ida Pearle and Joseph Cuba Community Archives and Genealogy Center of the William Breman Jewish Heritage Museum, Archivist Sandy Berman enthusiastically shared their collection with me. There I saw many family photographs of Leo and Lucille and held the leaflets that Leo prepared in prison and that Lucille typed for him at home. I saw the interview of Leo's nephew that Sandy had done in 2002. I read the schoolgirl diaries of a Birmingham, Alabama, teenager whose Jewish relatives had fled Atlanta after Governor Slaton's commutation order. Sandy even showed me Leo's desk and a catalog from the National Pencil Company—the collection even had an original pencil from the factory.

The Kenan Research Center, part of the Atlanta History Center, contained more newspaper articles and personal letters. Vice President, Research Services Paul Crater and Reference Manager Beth McLean were very helpful in having material ready for me in advance and in arranging for speedy photocopying. In addition to newspapers, I read letters that Leo and Lucille received from friends, offering sympathy and support and praising their steadfastness. I read loving letters from Lucille to Leo, letters from Leo's parents and letters from Lucille's parents—including the one Lucille's mother wrote to her while she was in Brooklyn for Leo's funeral, telling Lucille that she had Leo's wedding ring but could not give any particulars. Holding such a letter in my hand felt as if I were holding that ring, myself. To read Leo's and Lucille's writing was to feel as if I had met them and as if I had been entrusted to tell their story, fairly and honestly, as it had not been told in their lives.

I have tried to tell that story as justly and clearly as I could. I am indebted to my insightful critique group: Sandra Brug, Maurene J. Hinds, Kiri Jorgensen, and Linda Knox for their thoughtful reading and detailed comments; to the members of my previous critique groups: Marilyn D. Anderson, Judy Carney, Kristi Collier, Amanda Forsting, Michael Ginsberg, Elaine Hansen, Keiko Kasza, Barbara Larkin, Stuart Lowry, and Elsa Marston for their invaluable feedback on an early version of this book; to Kate Merkling for her critical early reading; and to John Merkling for vetting the manuscript through legal eyes. I'm grateful to Shannon Barefield for urging me to write this book, for patiently spending time in spirited discussions of my manuscript, and for leading me through revisions to make the story as clear and as precise as possible, since so many aspects of it are difficult to understand and express. I also appreciate Andrew Karre's thoughtful guidance through the final editing and launch of this book and his unfailing good humor as he introduced me to Microsoft Word, Facebook, and blogging. As always, my husband, Arthur B. Alphin, supported and encouraged me as I researched and pondered and wrote. He patiently listened to literally years of my analysis of the case and then took the time to read the manuscript and raise questions and offer feedback. I could not have written this book without him.

For me, the true thrill of research comes from doing more than reading books and newspapers. It comes from holding letters handwritten by real people. It comes from talking to archivists who actually knew the families I was writing about: one who was friends with one of Hugh Dorsey's grandsons and another who spent time with Leo's nephew. And it comes from seeing actual places. When I drove to Marietta, I thought I was prepared to see Tom Watson's lavish gravestone for Mary; and in fact, I walked almost instinctively straight to her grave. But I was shattered to see that gravestone crowded with teddy bears, just like any modern teenager's locker or gravesite. Many looked sun-faded, but others were quite recent, signs of grief that has never abated. Then I searched for the intersection that was the site of Leo's lynching and finally found a run-down building marked only by two small plaques that had carefully been positioned too high for easy vandalism.

Research transports me not only to another place but to another time. It brings the people of the past to life again, allowing me to introduce them to you, so that you can come to your own understanding of who they were and of what really happened in Atlanta in 1913.

SELECTED BIBLIOGRAPHY

Arnold, Reuben R. *The Trial of Leo Frank: Reuben R. Arnold's Address to the Court in His Behalf*. Baxley, GA: Classic Publishing Co., 1915.

Atlantic Publishing Co. *The Frank Case: Inside Story of Georgia's Greatest Murder Mystery*. Atlanta: Atlantic Publishing Co., 1913.

Auchmutey, Jim. "A Murder, a Lynching, a Mystery." *Atlanta Journal-Constitution*, June 11, 2000.

Bricker, Luther Otterbein. *Shane Quarterly*, April 1943, 89–95.

Brief of Evidence, Leo M. Frank v. State of Georgia, Supreme Court of Georgia at the October Term, 1913. Atlanta, 1913.

Busch, Francis X. *Guilty or Not Guilty?* Indianapolis: Bobbs-Merrill, 1952.

Connolly, C. P. "The Frank Case." *Collier's Weekly,* December 19, 1914, 6–24.

———. *The Truth about the Frank Case*. New York: Vail-Ballou Company, 1915.

Dinnerstein, Leonard. "The Fate of Leo Frank."*American Heritage* 47, no. 6 (October 1996): 98–109.

———. *The Leo Frank Case*. New York: Columbia University Press, 1968.

Dorsey, Hugh M. *Argument of Hugh M. Dorsey, Solicitor-General, Atlanta Judicial Circuit, at the Trial of Leo M. Frank, Charged with the Murder of Mary Phagan*. Macon, GA: N. Christophulos, n.d.

Frey, Robert Seitz, and Nancy C. Thompson. *The Silent and the Damned: The Murder of Mary Phagan and the Lynching of Leo Frank*. New York: Cooper Square Press, 2002.

Garrett, Franklin M. *Atlanta and Environs: A Chronicle of Its People and Events*. Vol. 2. Athens: University of Georgia Press, 1954.

Golden, Harry. *A Little Girl Is Dead*. New York: World Publishing Company, 1965.

Greene, Ward. *Death in the Deep South*. New York: American Mercury, 1938.

Gunther, John. *Taken at the Flood*. New York: Harper and Brothers, 1960.

Harris, Nathaniel E. *Autobiography of N.E. Harris*. Macon, GA: J. W. Burke Company Publishers, 1925.

Henson, Allen Lumpkin. *Confessions of a Criminal Lawyer*. New York: Vantage Press, 1959.

Hertzberg, Steven. *Strangers within the Gate City: The Jews of Atlanta, 1845–1915*. Philadelphia: Jewish Publication Society of America, 1978.

Lindemann, Albert S. *The Jew Accused*. Cambridge: Cambridge University Press, 1990.

Mamet, David. *The Old Religion*. New York: Free Press, 1997.

Melnick, Jeffrey. *Black-Jewish Relations on Trial: Leo Frank and Jim Conley in the New South*. Jackson: University Press of Mississippi, 2000.

Michael, Robert. *A Concise History of American Antisemitism*. New York: Bowman & Littlefield Publishers, 2005.

Oney, Steve. *And The Dead Shall Rise*. New York: Pantheon Books, 2003.

Phagan, Mary. *The Murder of Little Mary Phagan*. Far Hills, NJ: New Horizon Press, 1987.

Powell, Arthur G. *I Can Go Home Again*. Chapel Hill: University of North Carolina Press, 1943.

Rascoe, Burton. *The Case of Leo Frank*. Girard, KS: Haldeman-Julius Publications, 1947.

Samuels, Charles, and Louise Samuels. *Night Fell on Georgia*. New York: Dell Publishing, 1956.

Slaton, John M. *Commutation Order*. Atlanta, June 21, 1915.

Sutherland, Sidney. "The Mystery of the Pencil Factory." In *Ten Real Murder Mysteries—Never Solved!* New York: G. P. Putnam's Sons, 1929.

Todd, A. L. *Justice on Trial: The Case of Louis D. Brandeis*. New York: McGraw-Hill, 1964.

Van Paassen, Pierre. *To Number Our Days*. New York: Charles Scribners Sons, 1964.

Watson, Thomas W., ed. "The Celebrated Case of the State of Georgia vs. Leo Frank." *Watson's Magazine* 21, no. 4 (August 1915): 182–235.

Wilkes, Donald. "Wrongly Accused, Falsely Convicted, Wantonly Murdered." *Flagpole Magazine,* May 5, 2004, 7.

Wilson, Colin, and Damon Wilson. *Written in Blood: A History of Forensic Detection*. New York: Carroll & Graf Publishers, 2003.

Woodward, Vann. *Tom Watson: Agrarian Rebel*. New York: Macmillan Company, 1938.

OTHER PERIODICALS, 1913–1917

Atlanta Constitution, Atlanta Georgian, Atlanta Journal, Baltimore Jewish Com'T, Boston Herald, Boston Traveler, Brooklyn Citizen, Brooklyn Eagle, Florida Metropolis, Houston Post, Jeffersonian, Kansas City Star, Reno (NV) Gazette, New York Times, Oklahoman, Tuscaloosa (AL) Times-Gazette.

ARCHIVAL COLLECTIONS

Georgia Archives, Morrow, GA.

Georgia Newspaper Project, University of Georgia, Athens.

Leo Frank Collection, Atlanta History Center, Atlanta.

Leo Frank Collection, Emory University, Atlanta.

Leo Frank Collection, Ida Pearle and Joseph Cuba Community Archives and Genealogy Center of the William Breman Jewish Heritage and Holocaust Museum, Atlanta.

Leo Frank Collection, Jacob Rader Marcus Center of the American Jewish Archives, Cincinnati Campus, Hebrew Union College, Jewish Institute of Religion.

SOURCE NOTES

6   *Brief of Evidence, Leo M. Frank v. State of Georgia, Supreme Court of Georgia at the October Term, 1913* (Atlanta, 1913), 1.

6   Ibid.

9   Harold Ross, "The Leo M. Frank Case by a Reporter Who Studied the Tragedy" (San Francisco, June 23, 1915), Leo Frank Collection, American Jewish Archives, Cincinnati.

9   Luther Rosser and Herbert Haas, witness examination and legal depositions, 1913, Leo Frank Collection, American Jewish Archives, Cincinnati, 94–95.

11   *Atlanta Georgian*, April 30, 1913.

11   *Atlanta Constitution*, April 28, 1913.

12   Henry Alexander, *Some Facts About the Murder Notes in the Phagan Case* (Atlanta, 1914), 3–7.

12   *Atlanta Journal*, April 30, 1913.

12   Harold Ross, "The Leo M. Frank Case by a Reporter Who Studied the Tragedy," Leo Frank Collection, American Jewish Archives, Cincinnati.

14   Ibid.

15   *Brief*, 17.

15   Ibid., 202.

15   Ibid., 11.

17   Ibid., 17.

17   Ibid., 202.

17   Ibid.

19   *Atlanta Georgian*, August 18, 1913.

20   *Atlanta Constitution*, April 28, 1913.

21   *Atlanta Constitution*, September 13, 1914.

21   Ibid.

21   *Brooklyn Citizen*, January 1915.

24–25   Leo M. Frank to Lucille Frank, June 14, 1909, Leo Frank Collection, American Jewish Archives, Cincinnati.

25   *Atlanta Georgian*, June 15, 1913.

29   *Brief*, 27.

29   Ibid.

29   *Atlanta Journal*, April 28, 1913.

30   *Brief*, 209.

31   Ibid., 210.

33   *Atlanta Constitution*, April 30, 1913.

34   Luther Otterbein Bricker, *Shane Quarterly*, April 1943, quoted in Golden, 38, and Leonard Dinnerstein, *The Leo Frank Case* (New York: Columbia University Press, 1968), 33.

34   *Nashville Tennessean*, Sunday special section, March 7, 1982.

34   *Atlanta Journal*, April 29, 1913.

36   *Atlanta Constitution*, April 30, 1913.

36   *Atlanta Georgian*, June 15, 1913.

36   Lucille Frank to Thomas Loyless, September 28, 1915, Leo Frank Collection, American Jewish Archives, Cincinnati.

37   Ibid.

37   *Brief*, 216.

37   Ibid., 24.

37–38   Harry Golden, *A Little Girl Is Dead* (New York: World Publishing Company, 1965), 168.

38   Luther Otterbein Bricker, *Shane Quarterly*, April 1943, quoted in Golden, 38, and Dinnerstein, 33.

39   "Pinkerton Investigation Notes, 1913," Leo Frank Collection, American Jewish Archives, Cincinnati, 11.

40   *Atlanta Constitution*, May 1, 1913.

41   C. P. Connolly, *The Truth about the Frank Case* (New York: Vail-Ballou Company, 1915), 44.

42   *Atlanta Constitution*, May 6, 1913.

42   "Pinkerton Investigation Notes, 1913," Leo Frank Collection, American Jewish Archives, Cincinnati, 10.

42   Ibid., 11.

42   Ibid.

43   *Atlanta Constitution*, May 9, 1913.

43   Ibid.

43   Ibid.

43   "Pinkerton," 8–9.

43   Ibid., 19.

43   *Atlanta Constitution*, May 9, 1913.

45   *Atlanta Constitution*, May 10, 1913.

46   Ibid.

49   John M. Slaton, *Commutation Order*, Atlanta, June 21, 1915.

50   *Brief*, 283.

50   Slaton, *Commutation*.

51   *Brief*, 283.

51   Ibid., 289–291.

52   Ibid.

52   Rosser and Haas, 25.

53   *Atlanta Georgian*, July 13, 1913.

55   *Atlanta Georgian*, June 5, 1913.

55	*Atlanta Journal*, May 4, 1915.
56	*Atlanta Constitution*, June 5, 1913.
56	Ibid.
56	*Atlanta Georgian*, June 5, 1913.
56–57	Ibid.
57	Ibid.
58	Deposition of Dewey Hewell, Hamilton County, State of Ohio, 1913, American Jewish Archives, Cincinnati.
58	Steve Oney, *And The Dead Shall Rise* (New York: Pantheon Books, 2003), 88.
59	Rosser and Haas, 53–54.
59	*Atlanta Georgian*, July 14, 1913.
61	*Atlanta Journal*, July 28, 1913, quoted in Charles Samuels and Louise Samuels, *Night Fell on Georgia* (New York: Dell Publishing, 1956), 40.
61	Samuels and Samuels, 30; Dinnerstein, 60.
62	Donald Wilkes, "Wrongly Accused, Falsely Convicted, Wantonly Murdered," *Flagpole Magazine*, May 5, 2004, 7.
62	*Atlanta Journal*, July 28, 1913, quoted in Samuels and Samuels, 40.
65	*Atlanta Constitution*, July 28, 1913, quoted in Golden, 96, and Oney, 190.
65–66	*Brief*, 219.
66	Samuels and Samuels, 52.
66	*Atlanta Journal*, August 1, 1913.
66–67	*Brief*, 49.
67	Ibid., 46–47.
69	*Atlanta Georgian*, August 2, 1913.
69	*Brief*, 55.
71	Oney, 251.
72	*Atlanta Georgian*, August 6, 1913.
73	Hugh M. Dorsey, *Argument of Hugh M. Dorsey, Solicitor-General, Atlanta Judicial Circuit, at the Trial of Leo M. Frank, Charged with the Murder of Mary Phagan* (Macon, GA: N. Christophulos, n.d.), 146.
75	*Atlanta Journal*, August 12, 1913.
76	*Atlanta Constitution*, August 13, 1913.
78	*Atlanta Constitution*, August 14, 1913.
79	*Atlanta Journal*, August 14, 1913.
79	*Atlanta Constitution*, August 15, 1913.
80–82	*Brief*, 219.
82	Dorsey, *Argument of Hugh M. Dorsey*, 24.
82	Samuels and Samuels, 157.
82	Ibid., 159.
82	*Atlanta Georgian*, August 22, 1913.
82	Samuels and Samuels, 161.
83	Hugh M. Dorsey, quoted in Oney, 333.
83	Ibid.
83	Ibid.
83	Dorsey, *Argument of Hugh M. Dorsey*, 145–146.
85	Ibid.
85	*Atlanta Constitution*, August 26, 1913.
87	*Frank v. Mangum*, 237 U.S. 309 (1914).
87	Leo Frank to John Gould, October 29, 1914, Leo Frank Collection, American Jewish Archives, Cincinnati.
88	*Atlanta Georgian*, October 31, 1913.
88	*Kansas City Star*, January 17, 1915.
88	Leo Frank, leaflets, Ida Pearle and Joseph Cuba Community Archives and Genealogy Center of the William Breman Jewish Heritage and Holocaust Museum, Atlanta.
90	John Gunther, *Taken at the Flood* (New York: Harper and Brothers, 1960), 82.
91	Henry Alexander, *Some Facts About the Murder Notes in the Phagan Case* (Atlanta, 1914), 3–7.
91	Dinnerstein, 90.
93	*Atlanta Georgian*, March 13, 1914.
94	Albert Lasker to Leo Frank, November 23, 1914, Leo Frank Collection, Atlanta History Center.
95	Louis Marshall to Herbert Haas, December 21, 1914, Leo Frank Collection, Atlanta History Center.
95	*Atlanta Journal*, December 21, 1914.
95	*Frank v. Mangum*, 237 U.S. 309 (1914).
95	*Atlanta Journal*, May 10, 1915.
96	*Atlanta Journal*, November 22, 1914.
97	*Jeffersonian Magazine*, June 24, 1915.
97	*Atlanta Journal*, November 22, 1914.
97–98	Associated Press, March 15, 1914, box 2/11, American Jewish Archives, Cincinnati.
98	L. S. Roan to Luther Rosser et al, December 1914, in *Atlanta Journal*, April 20, 1915, and in *Atlanta Georgian*, May 31, 1915.
98	J. J. Barge to the Honorable Prison Commission and His Excellency, the Governor of Georgia, May 31, 1915, Leo Frank Collection, American Jewish Archives, Cincinnati.
99	*Jeffersonian Magazine*, March 19, 1914.

100   *Brooklyn Citizen*, September 2, 1913.

100   *Jeffersonian Magazine*, June 24, 1915.

100   *Reno (NV) Gazette*, December 23, 1914.

100–101 *Kansas City Star*, January 17, 1915.

102   Slaton, *Commutation*, 28.

103   *New York Times*, November 28, 1914.

103   *Boston Traveler*, June 1, 1915.

104   John M. Slaton, "The Frank Case," July 30, 1954, Ida Pearle and Joseph Cuba Community Archives and Genealogy Center of the William Breman Jewish Heritage and Holocaust Museum, Atlanta, 2.

105   *Atlanta Constitution*, October 3, 1914.

105–106 Marjorie Smith to anonymous, December 28, 1914, Leo Frank Collection, Atlanta History Center.

106   *Florida Metropolis*, June 21, 1915.

106–107 Slaton, *Commutation*, 28.

107   *Watson Magazine*, "The Celebrated Case of the State of Georgia vs. Leo Frank," August 1915, 235.

107   *Atlanta Constitution*, June 22, 1915.

107   *New York Times*, June 22, 1915.

107   Robert Seitz Frey and Nancy C. Thompson, *The Silent and the Damned: The Murder of Mary Phagan and the Lynching of Leo Frank* (New York: Cooper Square Press, 2002), 89–90.

109   *New York Times*, June 27, 1915.

109   *Boston Herald*, August 19, 1915.

110   Leo Frank to Rachel Frank, August 4, 1915, Leo Frank Collection, American Jewish Archives, Cincinnati.

110   Leo Frank to Lucille Frank, June 22, 1915, Leo Frank Collection, American Jewish Archives, Cincinnati.

111   Eleanore Stern to Leo Frank and Lucille Frank, mss 91, box 5, folder 2 and 3, Leo Frank Collection, Atlanta History Center.

111   *Tuscaloosa (AL) Times-Gazette*, June 21, 1915.

111–112 *Tuscaloosa (AL) Times-Gazette*, July 11, 1915.

112   Leo Frank to Lucille Frank, June 28, 1915, Leo Frank Collection, American Jewish Archives, Cincinnati.

112   *Baltimore Jewish Com'T*, July 23, 1915.

113   Ibid.

113   Lucille Frank, July 17, 1915, Leo Frank Collection, American Jewish Archives.

113   *Jeffersonian Magazine*, July 22, 1915.

115   *Oklahoma City Oklahoman*, July 20, 1915.

115   *Houston Post*, July 29, 1915.

115   *Baltimore Jewish Com'T*, July 23, 1915.

115   Herbert Haas to Lucille Frank, July 24, 1915, Leo Frank Collection, Atlanta History Center.

115   Leo Frank to Rachel Frank, August 4, 1915, Leo Frank Collection, American Jewish Archives, Cincinnati.

116   *New York Times*, August 19, 1915.

116   *Atlanta Constitution*, August 18, 1915.

118   *Augusta (GA) Chronicle*, August 23, 1915.

118   Ibid.

118   *New York Times*, August 19, 1915.

119   Ibid.

119   *Atlanta Journal*, August 17, 1915.

122   Ibid.

122   *Atlanta Georgian*, August 18, 1915.

122   *New York Times*, August 18, 1915.

122   *Brooklyn Eagle*, August 18, 1915.

122   *New York Times*, August 18, 1915.

122   Ibid.

124   *Public Affairs Press*, 1962, 60.

126   *Nashville Tennessean*, Sunday special section, March 7, 1982.

126   Ibid.

127–128 Ibid.

128   *Collier's: The National Weekly* 54, no. 15 (December 26, 1914), quoted in Connolly, 91–92.

130   *Augusta (GA) Chronicle-Herald*, May 15, 1983.

130   Georgia State Board of Pardons and Paroles, "Decision in Response to Application for Posthumous Pardon for Leo M. Frank," March 11, 1986.

131   *Atlanta Journal-Constitution*, January 6, 1999.

132   Pierre Van Paassen, *To Number Our Days* (New York: Charles Scribners Sons), 238.

133   Mary Phagan, *The Murder of Little Mary Phagan* (Far Hills, NJ: New Horizon Press, 1987), 226.

133   *Nashville Tennessean*, March 7, 1982.

INDEX

PHOTO ACKNOWLEDGMENTS

THE IMAGES IN THIS BOOK ARE USED WITH THE PERMISSION OF:

The Atlanta Georgian, (background image) pp. 1, 3, 5, 6, 9, 15, 21, 25, 27, 29, 34, 39, 45, 49, 55, 61, 73, 87, 97, 102, 110, 116, 117, 126, 135; (main image) pp. 27, 35; Photos courtesy of The Cuba Archives of the Breman Museum, Atlanta, GA, pp. 18, 22, 25, 32, 47, 53, 64, 68, 70, 75, 77, 79, 81, 84 (both), 86, 89, 91 (right), 92 (all), 98, 114, 121 (bottom), 125 (both), 126, 129, 135; New York Times Company Records, Adolph Ochs Papers, Manuscripts and Archives division, The New York Public Library, Astor, Lenox and Tilden Foundations, pp. 7, 46, 49, 58, 62–63 (all); Courtesy of Georgia Archives, Vanishing Georgia Collection, (BUR049) p. 8; (GWN150) p. 108; (BAL051) p. 120; (COB852) p. 121 (top); Courtesy of the Kenan Research Center at the Atlanta History Center, p. 10; © Bettmann/CORBIS, pp. 16, 91 (left), 113, 123 ; Atlanta Journal and Constitution, p. 39 (bottom); Library of Congress, (LC-USZ62-92298) p. 96; (LC-USZ62-130993) p. 99; Courtesy of Georgia Archives, Ad Hoc Collection, (LPC483), p. 102; © 1982, The Tennessean, p. 129.

Front cover: istockphoto.com/© paul kline (noose); Bettmann/Corbis (portrait of Leo). Back cover: Photo courtesy of The Cuba Archives of the Breman Museum, Atlanta, GA.